# The Bonsai Book
# of Practical Facts

JEROME MEYER

**A collection of brass tacks
tips and briefings for
novices and seasoned growers**

To my wife, Charlotte—for her generous
assistance and constructive criticism

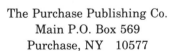

The Purchase Publishing Co.
Main P.O. Box 569
Purchase, NY   10577


1988

FOURTH PRINTING
Plus Addenda

**Library of Congress Cataloging-in-Publication Data**

Meyer, Jerome.
    The bonsai book of practical facts.

    Includes new material (addenda)
    Includes bibliographical references and index.
    1. Bonsai.    I. Title.
SB433.5.M49    1990                        635.9′772                        90-38869
ISBN 0-945487-00-2

Printed by Braun-Brumfield Inc.                    Photo credits: Charles Dembofsky
Composition by NK Graphics Inc.                                    John O'Donnell

10   9   8   7   6   5   4

Distributed in Australia and New Zealand by:
Books 'N' Things
228 Lennox Street
Richmond, Victoria 3121
Telephone: 03 427 0528

# Contents

## 4. Potting Soils

## 5. Trimming—Pruning—Pinching

pruning summary • Growth rates vary • Pinch all
sides • Grow and clip styling • Small leaves • Concealing a
new pruning scar • Shaping branches • Juniper branch
training • Creating a new branch • Styling never
ends • Winter shaping • Quick callus formation • When to
leave a branch alone • On thickening trunks • Grafting
trunks together • Thickening terminals • Creating foliage
close to trunks • Styling disaster • Growing tip
dilemma • Putting them out to graze • Timing the pruning
procedure • Growth habits • The penalty of
neglect • Maintenance trimming • Leaf pruning • Avoid
hasty pruning

## 6. Species Specifics                                      67

Climate orientation • Pines • Elms • Weeping
willow • Azalea • Yew (Taxus
varieties) • Junipers • Juvenile growth • EASTERN
REDCEDAR • Suitability for bonsai • Boxwood
varieties • Spruce species • Hinoki cypress • Flowering
crabapple • Maple varieties

## 7. The Wiring Ritual                                      77

Where to start • When to wire • When to avoid
wiring • Wiring hazards • Wire damage • Back branch
wiring • How to conceal blemishes through
wiring • Estimating wire length • Wiring caution • Tied
down branches • Branch-training timing • Broken branch
repair • Winterizing and wire • Annealing wire • What
annealing does • Aluminum wire • Removing
insulation • Removing wire • Trunk bending tip • Lost
branch • Straightening wire • Save tire weights • Wiring and
pinching • Wiring refresher

## 8. Containers                                             81

Mending broken pots • Training pots

## 9. Moss and Lichen                                        83

Browsing for moss and lichen • How to use it on your
bonsai • Applying lichen to trunks • It's not moss • Browning
moss • Cultivating ground covers • Mossing rock plantings

## 10. The Watering Dilemma

Facts of life • The timing factors • The daily watering regimen • The moisture compromise • What is "Overwatering?" • The rationale • Watering mechanics • Species variations • Wholesome neglect • Bonsai vs. houseplant watering • Watering and growth rate • Calculated risk • A choice of evils • Deep pot watering • Watering in the rain • Staggered watering • Winter watering • How to check drainage • Soil surface alert • Elevating containers • Leveling aids

## 11. Fertilizing

Organic vs. inorganic • Soil pH control • The meaning of pH • Plant pH requirements • Applying ashes • The end result • When to fertilize • Fertilizer concentrations • Rainfall and fertilizer • Fertilizer and wintering • Nutrition alternate • An early feeder • Acidifying soils • Last meal • Fertilizer basic • Fertilizing and potting soils • Hold the nitrogen • Feather rock hint • Yellowing foliage • Fertilizer choices • Note nitrogen sources • Slow-release fertilizers • Fertilizing rock plantings • Vague fertilizer instructions • Using proportional sprayers for fertilizers • Fertilizing summary

## 12. Winter Protection

Environmental changes • Winter protection objectives • Light and dormancy • Dormancy data • Dormancy variables • The meaning of winter-kill • Winter styling observations • Winter watering • Beware car exhaust • Wintering nursery material • Winter pruning and wiring • Horticultural spring • First wintering • Few bonsai to winter • Selecting nursery material • Drastic surgery • The cold treatment • Plants vs. humans • Wintering preparations • Wintering indoor bonsai • Ides of March • Terminating winter protection • Frost hazard

## 13. Pest Control

Timing the control • Spraying precautions • Three pest types • Insecticide types • Dormant oil sprays • Gypsy moth and tent caterpillars • Spider mites • Aphids • Mealybugs,

# Acknowledgments

Presented herein is a scenario of facts and an accumulation of data which I have assembled over a period of twenty years of bonsai culture. As Goethe once said, "Everything has been thought of before, but the problem is to think of it again."

This book is not intended to be a technical treatise on bonsai care and styling but, rather, a reference of fugitive ideas which, like the will-o'-the-wisp, occasionally come to mind and, just as quickly, depart. Capturing and documenting these facts results in this book. Some "Facts" have been derived from oral sources at bonsai meetings, lectures, seminars and symposia as well as comments from teachers and friends. Others were drawn from personal experience and some techniques described herein have never been explored before.

While I gleaned much of the information from my own material that first appeared in the *Yama Ki Newsletter*, of which I was editor for seven years, the only other documentation I have for *The Bonsai Book of Practical Facts* is my notebook and, sometimes, a reflection from the mirror of my mind. What evolved is a collage of ideas about bonsai.

For their inspiration and wholesome criticisms over the years, I am grateful to my teachers, Yuji Yoshimura and John Naka, among others. And for their often wry comments and observations, my genuine appreciation to a cadre of friends and fellow practitioners.

JEROME MEYER

Author's background: Past-president, The Bonsai Society of Greater New York; former editor, *The Bonsai Bulletin*; founder and past-president, Yama Ki Bonsai Society and editor of its *Newsletter*.

# *Foreword*

My intention in this work is to supply a collection of facts arranged in cyclopedic order covering essential functions of bonsai culture with emphasis on the two major aspects, *Care* and *Styling*. The purpose of these more than 400 detailed briefings is to furnish a storehouse of bonsai data adapted to address the problems that may be encountered, the objectives to be desired and the differences of opinion held by aficionados.

Procedures covering the horticultural artform of bonsai are replete with contradictions. This is evident in styling, fertilizing, soil mixes, containers, watering, winter protection, pest control—even the definitions of bonsai have their followers. The masters themselves often come head to head in opinions on what is correct.

In a large sense, differences of opinion reflect a matter of taste. It is no different in bonsai. Bonsai is not a science, but an art. A simple observation about styling, for example, may evoke a lot of conversation among the cognoscente. True, a small pot for a thin-trunked bonsai looks as absurd as a little hat on a big man, but there are those who have reasons for such disproportion in bonsai. Consider the bunjin style often used when none other will do and which usually ends up as an extreme design because it follows no standard styling rules. Who can say what is right or wrong in bonsai?

Bonsai is supposed to conjure up in the mind the image of a perfect tree in miniature, ideal and picturesque. All the rules coach and guide us to the realization of this perfection. "Idealizing" is relatively easy to accomplish if we recognize and follow the basics and eliminate styling features that violate the conceptions of "ideal." "Picturesque," however, is a matter of opinion. And there probably are as many versions of what is picturesque as there are masterful bonsai stylists.

Ask the uninitiated to recall a beautiful tree in nature and, invariably, the answer will be a tree that is old and gnarled, one that evokes a venerable picture in the mind of the observer. It probably will have rough bark excrescences, whitened driftwood, ramified, pendulous branches, thick, curved trunk, strong surface roots and evidence of abuse and adversity imposed by the elements. These are the features a casual observer may use to identify a beautiful tree in the woodland. These also are the very traits we try to achieve in bonsai which even one unfamiliar with bonsai goals will bring to mind.

It is the obvious old age of a tree that makes it memorable. In its natural surroundings, for a tree to *look* old it must *be* old; in bonsai, that appearance is accomplished by the styling techniques. In the graphic art representation of bonsai, however, the picture often is an exaggerated conception—a phantom illusion on paper which can never become a practical accomplishment.

We see many such illustrations of extravagantly styled bonsai. This is unfortunate because an enthused novice can easily be deceived. They hold out the promise of an aged, classical masterpiece in a few easy lessons. They are powerful drawings only—bonsai synthesized—rather than true representations of actual achievements. Exceptions to misleading illustrations of bonsai are the working drawings that picture a technical detail or solve a specific problem. These are blueprints for design, not phantom pictures of masterpieces that stimulate the desire for something that seldom can be fulfilled.

The inspiration that accompanies the practice of any art form makes us very vulnerable to the promise of quick success. When we start as novices with pencil-thick bonsai material and eventually succumb to more advanced nursery-grown stock, we realize the first call of discipline is patience. The learning process enables us, in time, to define what results are obtainable and which are beyond reach. Once the basics are learned, the imagination of the stylist takes over. Then bonsai becomes a creative art form in fact, not fancy.

All the bonsai pictured herein were styled by the author. Bonsai photographs, however, do not always present accurate measurement of depth and dimension. And photos sometimes deliver a distortion, too—a back branch that appears as if it originated from the side—or branches that appear crossed when, actually, they may be properly separated.

The photos illustrate good results and faulty ones—good plant material as well as specimens that leave something to be desired. Some "before" and "after" comparisons are presented to illustrate how simple alterations can convert unattractive traits to more harmonious forms or, through the techniques of concealing obvious faults, how styles can be improved. This work is not intended to be a picturebook of masterpiece bonsai. There are others that more than fulfill the promise. It is intended to be a practical critique of faults and aberrations frequently encountered and the ways and means to avoid them.

Technical language has been kept to a minimum. Wherever possible, identification of plant material is confined to common names.

The reader is assumed to be somewhat knowledgeable about bonsai, at least to the extent that bonsai is considerably more involved than merely putting a plant into a pot. The discipline, however, has so captured the imaginations of Americans, many individuals receive commercially-produced bonsai as gifts—like houseplants and they commonly keep the plants indoors. These little trees have critical cultural requirements. Indoor environments are hostile to many outdoor species used for bonsai. When their genetic needs are not met, they soon peter out. When they fail, it becomes a bitter disappointment.

*The Bonsai Book of Practical Facts* will gently guide the novice to the objectives of bonsai styling, care and culture. For the experienced grower, this book offers a quick refresher of basics plus hundreds of encyclopedic details not heretofore covered. To those who are strangers to bonsai and those who receive bonsai as gifts, this book could be the answer to a call for help.

# 1. *The Evolution of Bonsai*

Bonsai combines art and horticulture to produce a miniature of the perfect tree. Once the horticultural aspects are mastered, the rest becomes pure art.

The practice of growing miniature trees in pots flourished in China centuries before it was introduced in Japan. The Chinese collected from the wild, woody plant material with bizarre shapes which were transplanted into ornate containers. These ancient specimens probably were planted into pots that were oversize, too, in order to assure survival. We know little about the horticultural practices in those days but, inevitably, much trial and error must have endured before the collected trees survived root pruning and were miniaturized.

These potted specimens in China were called "artistic pot plants." Eventually the exotic shapes were further styled and enhanced through a training system known as "grow and clip" (the Lingnan School) in contrast to the Japanese who, centuries later, adopted copper wire to shape the specimens. As the Japanese expanded their civilization, they brought back these plants from China.

The earliest potted trees in Japan were not known as "bonsai" and the designation, meaning "tray tree," was not established until the practice increased in popularity. The evolution of bonsai is somewhat vague and, as living objects, were lost in antiquity in marked contrast to the artifacts of Greece and Rome which survived and from which we can document the cultural history.

It is fairly certain, however, that the bonsai beginning in Japan was characterized, like the Chinese, by the collection of trees dwarfed naturally, contorted by wind and erosion. The early Japanese were satisfied with putting these specimens into containers and enjoying them as nature in the raw—the older and more picturesque the better.

The material was carefully selected and plants with contorted and twisted trunks were highly prized. It became legend that aged trees, having endured hardship, were much to be desired. "Surviving adversity" was a characteristic sought and selected. Since the Japanese loved things in miniature, they were captivated with these diminutive trees.

No attempt was made to style and refine these natural shapes as we know the artform today. The rugged and primitive forms were sufficient. In time, easily collectible material from the mountains and forests was virtually exhausted, much in the same way our own Western species growing wild and suitable for bonsai culture are now becoming few and far between. It is not difficult to visualize that the Japanese landscape, a small fraction of what we have in America, was soon denuded of natural material.

**Supply and demand.** As naturally dwarfed plants from the wild became scarce, the Japanese started plants from seed and cuttings, selected specimens from their gardens and acquired nursery stock to convert into bonsai. Then someone got the inspiration—"Why not shape and style these cultivated imitations to simulate trees growing naturally—to amplify their natural beauty and give them an aged look like those in the wilderness?" That started it all—the styling, the perfection, the refinement. They did it with the aid of *wire* to freeze in reality the shapes that the imagination pictured in their minds.

There is evidence that the Japanese sometimes went to great extremes to improve their bonsai and that some of the specimens reputed to be hundreds of years old actually were artificially carved and gouged and totally reconstructed. Of course, countless years of growth have obscured these alterations, but it indicates the extremes the forebears of bonsai explored, in addition to the techniques of bending and wiring trunks and branches, to reach for perfection.

That, in brief, is the evolution of bonsai. It is quite likely the Japanese considered bonsai cultivation as an art indulged by the leisure class—a vehicle to duplicate nature in miniature just as the exquisitely fashioned ivory carvings (netsuke) depict people and situations in every day life.

**Migration to America.** In the late 1940's, troops stationed in Japan as the Army of Occupation scoured the countryside for artifacts, hand-carved jade and ivory figures, ceremonial swords and other treasures. Some of our boys encountered rare bonsai which, in the Japanese tradition, had been handed down from generation to generation. Since the bonsai culture in Japan was strictly a male preoccupation and with men to war, the trees were neglected. Many disappeared.

Some of these rare finds were brought back to America. A few survived quarantine and fumigation by the U.S. Department of Agriculture. Americans fell in love with them.

In the 1950's, many Japanese gardening and plant specialists came to America and settled in California. These immigrants, steeped in the bonsai tradition, filled in the gaps of bonsai information.

Americans, hungry for authentic bonsai knowledge, were eager to learn. The Japanese-Americans provided the answers through classes, lectures and demonstrations, first through their own ethnic sections in California, later through the Middle-west and the East. The culture of little trees spread to almost everyone with a variety of green thumb and a flair for art. It was not long before bonsai became a near obsession to plant lovers almost everywhere.

And, thus, bonsai was introduced to America, barely forty-five years ago.

# 2. *The Bonsai Mystique*

**Definitions.** The art and aim of bonsai has had many interpretations. The early definitions included words like "stunted" or "dwarfed" in the sense of the Chinese versions of antiquity. This was unfortunate because such descriptions imply disfigurement. Bonsai simply are little trees in pots miniaturized through natural means. They possess every characteristic of their counterparts growing in nature. They never can be considered misshapen or grotesque.

As mentioned previously, the literal translation of bonsai from the Japanese is "tray tree." After bonsai gained popularity in America, other identifications were assigned by the cognoscente including such lyrical descriptions as *living sculpture* and the *four dimensional artform*. Serious growers also developed their own esoteric descriptions and *horticultural artform* became a popular designation. Finally, *a tree in a pot that resembles a tree in nature* appeared to capture the sense and meaning of these miniature trees—and this became the generic description adopted by the bonsai community.

None of these descriptions, however, manages to picture bonsai styling goals—the end result—even if the end result may actually be years away. A definition should leave no room for doubt.

**Unlocking the answer.** True, bonsai is a "tray tree." Almost any species of woody plant material may be grown in a container. With proper care and cultivation, it may flourish as a "tree in a pot." As for "living sculpture," what other horticultural interest involves such skillful use of the pruning shears, scissors, wood-carving tools, wire, weights and paraphernalia?—skillful in the sense that one must know where and how much to cut and shape, and when. Bonsai as "living sculpture" tells more about the technique we study, learn and, eventually, apply in styling.

That bonsai is "four dimensional" cannot be denied. Time is the one dimension that separates bonsai from other art forms. Bonsai does not assume harmony and character overnight. Once a plant has been shaped and wired, the tree looks scraggly and incomplete. When we administer styling attention and care, even in a single season's development, a miraculous change takes place.

"Horticultural artform," an apt description, is much too vague a definition. While it emphasizes the skills involved, it still falls short of the mark. This description also can apply to topiary, espalier, ornamental gardening, ikebana, or flower arranging. Once the designs have been established, these projects are finished. Not so with bonsai. The styling goes on forever.

That bonsai is "A tree in a pot resembling a tree in nature" comes close, but not quite. Nature is not programmed for esthetics, unsymmetrical balance or harmony—all styling factors inherent in the bonsai technique. A driftwooded tree in nature is the result of a disaster. In bonsai, driftwood is part of the styling scheme and deliberately built in where appropriate. Artifice thus becomes one of the requisites.

Propagation of the species is nature's purpose. Nature overproduces to assure survival. More branches are grown than necessary in order to provide an abundance of leaves with which to produce ample food, whereas in bonsai we actually eliminate branches to create "style." In order to make certain there will be enough, nature is wasteful; in bonsai, we are thrifty. If you just aim to imitate nature, you will have only a "tree in a pot," not bonsai.

**The ultimate definition.** What we aim to imitate in nature are the characteristics that suggest *idealism* and *picturesque age*. The sense and spirit of bonsai are typified through these characteristics. *Ideal* is process—*picturesque*, the goal. Together, they are bonsai *technique*, which converts a simple, woody "tree in a pot" to something elegant—a perfect miniature tree in a pot that resembles an *idealized and picturesque tree in nature*. And that is where the bonsai description ends.

## What is Ideal?

An "ideal" tree results from following some simple rules given to us by the Japanese masters who developed them after years of bonsai styling and observation. Some rules seek to avoid artistic compromise; others were established for reasons of plant health and horticulture. Always, the rules represent guidelines for "ideal"—elimination in styling of the generic traits considered unattractive and the adoption of those traits in nature that enhance a tree's beauty.

Every element of bonsai styling was taken into account by these Japanese forebears in order to replicate a small but perfect tree growing in a container. These styling elements include proportions, branch configuration and positioning—synthesis of aging characteristics, plus container sizes, shapes and colors—even placement of the plant in a pot. Gradually, these styling rules became exacting standards of the bonsai discipline. Thus, the rules the Japanese left as a legacy help us to reach for perfection because they eliminate the traits that contradict perfection.

"Idealizing," then, is accomplished by recognizing that certain rules do exist, that bonsai is not just a matter of "putting a plant in a pot." By emphasizing the rules, we also enhance the effect.

**Artistic choices often the most natural.**   Ideally, a bonsai silhouette should be in the shape of a triangle, preferably of unequal sides, to conform to the traditional Japanese philosophy. We attempt to form a three-sided figure with the apex, sides and bottom plane. To the Japanese, this represents heaven, earth and man.

Pyramidal and conical trees growing in nature do have a triangular configuration, but the elms, oaks, willows and locusts grow from broad crowns and no apexes. We have learned from experience and from observation of finished, classical bonsai that the triangular configuration is what we should follow for authentic practice of the art.

**Nature violates bonsai rules for "ideal."**   We see opposite branching in nature all the time, but the Japanese avoid this because it is considered a "juvenile" trait; hence, opposite branches or "bar branches" are to be avoided. One branch directly over another (parallel branching) also is taboo because the lower branch ultimately will be shaded and eventually die back. So parallel branches should be wired to grow in different planes.

Spoke-wheel branching, so common in many pine species, should be avoided by pruning away all branches but one, although an additional "spoke" can remain as a back branch if there is no other choice. Crossing branches are confusing to the eye so they, too, are eliminated or straightened by wire to remove the aberration. Then there are the branch ends. Branches ending

*A venerable oak, approximately 500 years old, with prominent features we try to duplicate in bonsai—as well as elements we try to avoid such as opposite branches, parallel branching and a heavy branch pointing upward. We attempt to replicate in bonsai the traits that represent "ideal" and enhance the characteristics that typify "picturesque"—which ultimately culminates in a perfect fusion of art and technique.*

in a U are unrealistic because a branch should have a distinct terminal at the end of it the same as the trunk.

Similarly, branches growing straight up or straight down should be removed, as well as those growing inward because nature would never tolerate the existence of such branches for long without the benefit of sunlight. They violate our vision of "ideal" as do twigs growing from internodes and crotches—because, ideally, twigs grow along branches.

"Idealizing" also suggests branch locations on the trunk. Wherever possible, a branch should start from a convex trunk curve rather than concave. While the latter occurs in nature, it is unrealistic in bonsai. "Idealizing" means a tapered trunk from roots to the terminal even if a surrogate terminal was skillfully created with a suitable branch growing upward and wired into position to continue the trunk line.

**Stick to the guidelines.** According to one Japanese master, Americans are more inclined to a "free form" bonsai rather than be pinned down to observance of classical guidelines for styling. Usually, however, "free form" in any art suggests an indifference to the rules rather than a new spirit or creative process. Learning classical rules to make bonsai "ideal" is intellectually taxing and it usually takes some little time to realize the rules were right. It is so much easier to "do your own thing."

There's really no challenge when you create bonsai just to imitate a tree in nature. You simply put it in a pot and watch it grow. You would ignore the rules— painstakingly arrange for opposite branching, crossing branches, parallel branches, branches terminating in a U and lower branches bent upward. But the rules tell us to beware of these esthetic faults, even if they often are apparent in trees growing in the wilderness—because they do not represent perfection.

So bonsai must be *idealized*—a veritable caricature where, in time, a few branches on a trunk are so placed and positioned that they tell a complete story—an illusion of the perfect, genuine article that becomes accessible. Only by following the man-made guidelines, which sometimes conflict with nature's own, can we approach the ideal.

## The Mental Image of "Picturesque"

Picturesque stirs a feeling within us of charm and beauty. In a tree, this mental image usually implies one that is old. Even a person who knows nothing about trees can tell the difference between a young tree and an old one.

*Picturesque* identifies the elements that evoke age— driftwood trunks—forsaken trees that braved adversity and survived, branches bleached and broken into jagged ends as if they were struck by lightning (jin)—exfoliating bark and fissures—bark peeled away from traumatized trunks showing whitened heartwood (shari)— a trunk thicker at the bottom and tapering to the top. These are the clues of a venerable woodland native and we craft into bonsai the same picturesque appearance of deprivation and antiquity.

**Signs of old age.** In natural surroundings, Ponderosa pine has a bark color which is almost black; when the tree gets between eighty and one-hundred years old, the bark turns brown. Short-lived birch, old at forty, is gray when young and, when about twenty years old, turns white. And the branches of Norway spruce droop only after the tree reaches twenty-five and older.

In bonsai, the actual age of a tree is not nearly as important as the age we make it appear. The age characteristics are by-products of bonsai design. These traits— defiance, hardship, struggle—are built in artificially to conjure up in the observer's mind a true representation of picturesque age in a tree. Seldom, if ever, do we acquire material for styling with *ideal* and *picturesque* characteristics in place. Sometimes, while collecting material from the wild, we can find a specimen that actually is, and looks, old in years, but this is rare.

Gnarled branches, and their positions, also are obvious signs of age. Young branches on top of the tree reach for the sun, so they are wired upward; lower branches should be pendulous and wired downward to create the illusion that, by sheer weight, they have grown in that direction—old and heavy.

We pinch and trim branch ends because we want ramification with twigs and twiglets to suggest oldness; healed scars, blemishes and calloused surfaces suggest that the tree had a hard life—and that's a sign of old age no one can deny.

We try to capture through styling the telltale evidences of long life. The shape of the trunk is one sure sign. Twisted trunks are a natural phenomenon; straight trunks are characteristic of saplings. Even a very young specimen, with a straight and uninteresting trunk, can be made to appear old and curved by training it with wire. If the trunk lacks a feeling of maturity, the illusion is incomplete; if the trunk is curved and graceful, this is picturesque. So the shape of the trunk can be altered to convey picturesque age in nature (see Photo Sequence #1).

We purposely create jin and weathered driftwood to mirror nature's hardships and imperfections; we expose surface roots as if eroded by time; we try to acquire material with rugged bark—smooth bark implies immaturity. We want no suggestion that this specimen is not a forest native—even if the subject actually is young in age but old in the appearance we have built into it.

Call this deception, or artifice, if you will—but this is the art of bonsai. (CONTINUED ON PAGE 15)

### PHOTO SEQUENCE #1
Juniper Shimpaku, Juniperus chinensis var Sargentii,
22-inches tall, potted 1979 from nursery stock.

*This specimen originally was potted as an informal upright ("Before"). The terminal was jinned and the surrogate terminal was formed from a thick branch growing upward. While the trunk is too thin for the tree height, the generous branching provides "mass" for informal upright styling. The bonsai was trained in this position for several years and foliage "clouds" started to develop.*

*The terminal direction was changed with the aid of heavy No. 6 wire ("After"). Since the wire was impossible to bend with the fingers, an adjustable pliers was engaged at various levels around the trunk and used as a lever. This resulted in better informal upright styling with the terminal directly over the base. The branches were wired parallel to the soil surface with branch ends pointing upward. Since the unfortunate curve in the terminal was eliminated, the trunk assumed a realistic continuity and the jinned portion became more visible.*

BEFORE                                           AFTER

**Reaching for the stars.** The final beauty of bonsai lies in training which probably never ends. This does not suggest that there is no compromise. Bonsai can be groomed, wired and trained continuously—to whatever stage of perfection the grower envisages. A great sense of satisfaction can be attained even if the bonsai is a degree or two below the styler's expectations. At some point there must be a happy medium. Following the rules slavishly may lead to disappointment and frustration.

Simply wiring branches down and avoiding the glaring faults will convey the conception of "ideal" and, sooner or later, the rules will become automatic. The element of "picturesque," however, cannot be similarly simplified. That's where artistry shines.

If you are content with a tree or shrub grown naturally and without the classic shape and air of an *ideal* and *picturesque* result, then there is no problem and "a tree in a pot" provides sufficient satisfaction. In skillful hands, even a young tree can impart a feeling of great age when the fundamentals are applied. If you yearn to reach for the stars, bonsai must represent an *improvement* over nature—a tree-in-a-pot with an illusion of perfection—*ideal* and *picturesque*.

### PHOTO SEQUENCE #2
### Trident maple, Acer buergeranum,
### 22-inches tall, potted 1981 from field-grown stock.

*The most desirable feature about this unfortunate specimen is the strong surface rootage, evenly distributed around the base. The disturbing left branch, pointing upward, is impossible to lower without drastic re-construction. The surrogate terminal created from the branch will never "catch up" in thickness to the original trunk. Some improvement is apparent in the "after" photo as a result of moderate wiring, but this is an example of inadequate stock selection with discouraging design flaws that are difficult to correct.*

BEFORE

AFTER

# 3. *The Birth of a Bonsai*

Plant material for converting into bonsai can be acquired from several different sources. Your own backyard or new housing developments can represent a treasure trove of potential bonsai in the way of abandoned landscaping specimens. Foundation plantings that have outgrown their space can be replaced with new nursery stock and the original planting can be used for bonsai. Remember, bonsai can be styled from trees, shrubs or vines—any woody material that can be shaped, pruned and wired. Sometimes a potential masterpiece can be found in places where you least expect it.

Material purchased in haste can often be disappointing when it comes to eventual styling (see Photo Sequence #2). Don't be impulsive when making selections. Evaluate the important design elements (see "Order of Importance," page 15). Some attractive features of a specimen, a thick trunk for example, can end up as a problem. Generous trunk proportions can be deceiving if other styling elements are missing or if an obvious fault in structure requires extensive surgery that would take years of growth to overcome.

Well-established nurseries offer a wide variety of material suitable for conversion into bonsai. It is best to stick with material that is readily available and with the species most commonly used for bonsai. Try to acquire species with small leaves or needles that are in better scale to true miniatures. The most popular choices are the various juniper varieties, pines, spruces and other conifers—the deciduous species such as native maple, elm, zelkova, hornbeam and fruiting trees—as well as the shrubs, such as azalea, cotoneaster, pyracantha and serissa.

Larger specimens are "balled and bagged." Other nursery stock is grown in cans ranging in sizes from half-gallon capacity to two or three-gallon sizes. The larger the nursery can, the older the plant material and the more complex will be the styling. Remember, material acquired from nurseries is not intended specifically for bonsai, but to supply landscaping needs for gardens. These nurseries purchase plant material from sources far and wide and some of the plants they sell may be of doubtful hardiness when eventually transplanted into a pot. They may be perfectly suitable for in-ground temperatures but, once the root zone of some plants is exposed to air temperature in a lower temperature zone, the plant may not survive. This also applies to over-wintering nursery material in cans or balled and bagged.

Vendors at bonsai conventions and seminars, or at meetings of bonsai societies, are one of the best sources for pre-bonsai material. These vendors instinctively eliminate those species that are not appropriate for bonsai and this may be a help to novices. Many vendors also offer pre-bonsai stock, often already in containers, sometimes shaped and trained. This is an important factor for those who want to get a head start.

Finally, there is collecting from the wild, an expedition into suitable areas (with permission, of course) where established specimens can be acquired for further development, training and styling (see "Collecting from the Wild," page 115). Material collected from one Hardiness Zone and transplanted to another often fails to respond with the same growth habit. It is better to collect from the same geographical area as the place where the bonsai will be trained and maintained. (See "Climate Orientation," page 67).

**Material evaluation.** When selecting potential bonsai material, determine whether the plant has at least one distinguishing feature. Inasmuch as many branches will have to be sacrificed, look for a profusion of branches and a choice of branch thicknesses. Unless a nursery specimen has irresistible features such as a thick and tapered trunk, strong surface roots or exfoliating bark, it will present a design problem if it lacks ample branching. Choices must be made and there are priorities in the elements of every potential bonsai. Since you will be working on the material for a long time and caring for it as you would a pet, devote time and attention to inspection before you invest your time and effort.

The various growth elements have a priority based on the impressions they deliver to the viewer as to "ideal" and "picturesque." Each observer may be influenced by different factors and, likewise, each bonsai master has a different concept of what is important. The criteria are practical considerations: Which elements are replaceable through growth, how long will it take, which parts are needed for styling and which can be sacrificed and are expendable?

Each component of a tree must be taken into account when making an evaluation of material to be converted to bonsai. To what extent does each portion contribute to the vision of a perfect, picturesque result? Based on this concept, it's *first* the roots—*second* the trunk—*third* the branches—*fourth* the foliage. These are the most desirable qualities rated on how effectively they communicate.

**Strong surface roots.**    An impressively buttressed trunk with prominent surface roots communicates a feeling of age at first glance (see Photo Sequence #3). In nature, buttressed roots stabilize a tree. The taller the tree and the thicker the trunk, the more pronounced the buttressing structure should be. In time, these buttressed roots become bark-like. While many old trees do lack conspicuous roots above ground, this characteristic generally is associated with immature trees and saplings.

Ideally, surface roots should be heavy and strong, radiating around the base as if the tree were anchored by them. Check for good roots below the soil surface, too. Very often they are concealed by a top layer of unimpressive roots which can be removed. Surface roots must be there before you start to style. Almost never will impressive surface roots develop in a container in contrast to the growth rate of branches and foliage.

Surface Roots, when available, should be positioned around the pot, but roots cannot be replaced or started from scratch. There are techniques for grafting, but the result is unreliable, risky and time-consuming. The high priority of "roots" in Order of Importance does not suggest that potential bonsai material would be worthless if surface roots were lacking. On the contrary, the candidate for styling or for purchase may have other very desirable qualities; but surface roots are considered paramount and not replaceable. Even if surface roots are scanty and precious little, they are better than none at all.

**Impressive trunk.**    The limiting factor in styling is the trunk and this is the next most desirable asset. To a large degree, however, this is reversable. An uninteresting trunk can be altered with heavy wire or by bending with a jack devised for this purpose.

Generous trunk girth communicates age the same as the roots and, if the trunk shows exfoliating bark, so much the better. Ideally, the trunk should be flaired from the soil surface and tapered all the way to the terminal. A trunk can appear to be thicker if the bonsai is styled shorter. Squat, thick bonsai are highly coveted among experienced growers (see Photo Sequence #4).

Trunk girth of a plant growing in a pot will hardly be noticeable although bonsai planted on rocks will expand quickly due to the heat of the sun held by the rock (see Photo #5). Nothing much can be done to a thick, unbendable trunk by way of shape except to wait for nature to age it. With junipers and other conifers, jin and shari (see page 38) can be created to enhance the aging appearance.

**The branches.**    Branches are third in priority in material selection. Like the trunk, they can be altered. If weak and uninteresting, branches can be encouraged to grow vigorously and they can be wired according to the state of the art into acceptable shapes. In time, branches can be replaced. Every new bud on a trunk is a potential new branch and, often, it is just a matter of deciding which bud is in the best position. In some species, such as azalea, experienced growers often prune away all branches and select new growth for the permanent structure.

**The foliage.**    This is the last in the sequence because it is the easiest element on which to compromise. If the plant is vigorous, rich foliage will develop in one growing season. If the leaves or needles are larger than desired, they will diminish in size during a plant's tenure in a pot.

Species with small leaves such as Catlin elm, Chinese elm or serissa are preferred. We would hardly select material for bonsai such as horse chestnut or tulip tree with leaves larger than the size of a person's hand. Small leaves or needles and rough bark are genetic characteristics and depend largely on the plant species. While foliage diminishes in size over the years in a pot, fruit and flowers remain the same size.

**Summary.**    Roots are the first in Order of Importance followed by trunk, branches and foliage. You may not have all the choice features in every specimen you tackle or every finished bonsai you may consider for purchase, but the discerning eye will select plant material that has one or two distinguished characteristics.

An exception occurs when you acquire collected material from the wild where an opportunity for extensive alteration is limited. Such material often grows badly asymetrical with scanty branching on one side and ponderous branches on the other which then presents styling problems. Sometimes surface roots are lacking and trunks are too straight for maximum interest. There is no guarantee, just because they grow naturally, that natural specimens offer ideal perfection.

Nevertheless, collected material usually conveys a rugged feeling compared with nursery or field grown stock. Branches develop heavier in the wild and may become very impressive. Many bonsai are styled with (CONTINUED ON PAGE 21)

## PHOTO SEQUENCE #3
### Korean boxwood, Buxus microphylla,
### 16-inches tall, potted 1976 from nursery stock.

*Strong surface roots are the most striking characterictic of this bonsai. The soil is mounded too high for the container depth ("Before"). The tree subsequently was potted lower in the container without sacrificing exposed surface roots ("After"), the branches were thinned and the pot centered under the foliage for a more pleasing balance.*

**BEFORE**

**AFTER**

PHOTO SEQUENCE #4
Trident maple, Acer buergerianum,
18-inches tall, potted 1980 from nursery stock.

*Massive, buttressed trunks, so highly coveted by many experienced stylists, often present problems from the standpoint of design. One of these problems is handling the terminal where a tall, thick trunk was amputated to bring the plant down to size. The maple above is a typical example of this dilemma ("Before").*

*A branch was fortuitously situated pointing upward, however, and this was wired into position. Nevertheless, the relative thickness of the trunk continuation remained awkward. Since maples and other deciduous species are apical dominant, they quickly develop prominent crowns rather than distinct terminals. In the bonsai pictured, the foliage at the top was allowed to grow without pruning branchlets. The resulting canopy of foliage conceals the contrasting thickness between the trunk and the new terminal. In addition, branches growing along the surrogate terminal have helped to thicken it.*

*The trunk also features an unfortunate "tunnel," a growth characteristic of the species. This fault was camouflaged by positioning the tree in the pot so it was not prominently visible. The opening also was packed with soil and planted with lichen. The blemish is not apparent from the front view.*

*Trimmed and wired ("After"). Left branch was more clearly outlined. Some foliage was allowed to remain over the straight portion of the trunk with a "see through" effect. Usually, no branches should pass in front of the trunk halfway up. A slight deviation of this rule serves the purpose of concealing a fault without disrupting the trunk line. The terminal canopy also was reduced and here, again, branchlets were wired across the upper trunk to veil the point of amputation.*

*Pictured, also, is the same bonsai during winter dormancy.*

BEFORE                    AFTER                    DEFOLIATED

PHOTO #5
Five-needle pine on rock, Pinus parviflora sp.,
27-inches tall, styled 1976 from nursery stock and seed.

*The rock is volcanic material carved by the author to simulate a Chinese "river rock." Two smaller rocks were cemented together to acquire height. Volcanic rock is relatively easy to carve with a dull instrument such as an old screwdriver and hammer. The openings and serpentine channels were shaped with a chisel.*

*The main tree, with a one-inch trunk diameter, and the left bottom tree were nursery grown. The other two specimens were grown from seed.*

*Bonsai planted on black rock grow vigorously. Heat retained by dark material stimulates root growth and the top responds. The main tree was pencil-thick when the group was assembled—one-inch thick when photographed.*

*The porous volcanic rock, formed by solidification of molten magma or lava, retains considerable moisture.\* This planting is kept in good color and vigor with watering once daily and five hours daily of sun exposure.*

*The soil surface consists of a peat muck layer which is replenished with fresh peat muck every two years to replace that lost through erosion, then covered with lichen growing on garden loam.*

*The roots penetrate through the rock and, occasionally, can be observed extending through the openings. They are trimmed away. The group never has been dismantled or otherwise root pruned.*

---

*A similar rock weighing 35.7 lbs. was soaked in a tub of water for thirty minutes until air bubbles disappeared, indicating saturation. The rock was drained in the shade for another thirty minutes and weighed again. The final weight was 38.5 lbs. indicating 2.8 lbs. of water retention or 7.84%.

such a feature as a focal point (see Photo #6). Think twice before you prune away a thick, prominent branch even if it is somewhat out of position.

**The ultimate compromise.** Try to make do with the material at hand. It would be bonsai Utopia if every one of the features in "Order of Importance" were present in every specimen you inspect. While every bonsai stylist yearns for the perfect combination, skills are honed through working with something less than ideal. Even the most experienced have learned to compromise with a flaw here and there—a compromise that seldom diminishes the satisfaction experienced through the eyes of the beholder.

Even after years of training, it is not always possible for every element to fall into perfect alignment. Sometimes it is necessary, in the interest of perfection, to "cover up." We discreetly wire branches to hide an imperfection or carelessness in styling; we insert rocks to detract from an obvious lack of surface roots. (See Photo Sequence #12). The untrained eye probably will never notice a slight diversion from what we consider ideal.

But it is there nevertheless. Deception thus becomes part of the artform concealing a flawed design feature that might be apparent to a knowledgeable observer. The "cover up" is a valid subterfuge from the "bag of tricks"—a simple wiring and bending, or a prudently placed rock—all part of the bonsai skill.

## The First Potting

The first potting is the most critical because it invariably involves extensive remodeling of the roots from nursery or field-grown stock. Re-potting from a plant already conditioned to a container (see "Re-potting," page 42) is relatively easy unless the roots are copious and long neglected. Many novices exaggerate the risk of handling roots and view the first potting procedure with trepidation. Even individuals thoroughly experienced with house plants, who think nothing of cutting back the top of the plant, become resistant when it comes to severing the roots. This is a natural obsession, but it needn't be when common sense and moderation are the guidelines. Root pruning prior to potting is just another routine phase of bonsai culture.

Merely lifting a mature plant out of the ground or transferring it from a nursery can into a bonsai container or training pot can drastically alter its environment. There is bound to be a certain amount of stress which, in a plant, translates into shock. In addition, the growing conditions are modified. Moisture requirements change—and so does light as well as soil and drainage. Plants usually compromise with these changes and they recover no worse for wear. The older the material, however, the greater the hazard.

When old, established material, whether nursery-grown or collected, is considered for bonsai, it is best to plan the operation by stages. First, do the preliminary styling and wiring. Then, a month or two later, tackle the actual potting.

Seedlings or young saplings or plants started from cuttings suffer very little when their environments are changed to containers, but ultimate maturity to creditable bonsai takes much longer to achieve.

**The potting schedule.** Deciduous bonsai are potted first when the buds are swollen, but before the leaves emerge. This is most important for apples and other fruiting species. After leaves emerge, it may be too late. Next in line are other deciduous species such as maples and elms. Then come the pines and spruces and, last, junipers when new growth is apparent. Azaleas and other flowering species are potted after flowering which may come as late as the middle of May. Remove the flowers and seedheads of azalea to conserve nourishment for the rest of the plant.

**Material required.** Assemble all components before you start the potting operation. Avoid suspending the procedure to hunt for a tool, pot or soil. Even a short exposure to dry air or wind may dehydrate delicate root hairs. Have everything at your finger tips including:

1. Concave pruners for branch removal.
2. Old pruning shears for pruning roots. New shears get dull quickly on contact with soil.
3. Chopstick or pointed dowel for working soil around roots.
4. Root tool for separating roots from root ball.
5. Small scissors for trimming branchlets.
6. Large scissors for trimming fibrous roots (household scissors will do).
7. Copper wire for securing rootball, #18 or #20. Thinner wire gauges for making last minute wiring corrections.
8. Pliers for pulling wire through rootball.
9. Wire cutter.
10. String for securing plant while working and supporting.
11. Plastic screens for covering drainage holes.
12. Wide brush for smoothing soil surface.
13. Moss or lichen for finishing soil surface.
14. Water spray bottle to keep roots moistened.
15. Towel.
16. Bonsai or training pot (flower pot, azalea pot or plastic pot).
17. Prepared soil.
18. Small scoop.

PHOTO #6
Ponderosa pine, Pinus ponderosa,
21-inches tall, potted 1969 from collected material.

*An effective style change could have been considered for this bonsai by amputating the powerful, protruding right branch and converting the tree to a semi-cascade style. Rotating the specimen 45° counter-clockwise could have positioned the twisted trunk into an ideal semi-cascade version.*

*Such strong branches, even when out of position, should not casually be cut away despite a design flaw. The branch is old and plated with exfoliating bark. It also serves to interrupt a somewhat straight trunk. The Japanese have great respect for a thick, old branch. They try to preserve such an "icon of respect for age" even if it is somewhat out of place in the scheme of bonsai design.*

*Think twice before you sacrifice such a branch. The styling rules can be stretched when obvious faults are encountered in old, collected material.*

PRELIMINARY STYLING

The purpose of preliminary styling is to expose the most attractive elements of the plant to full view and shape the trunk and branches for future development. Start with the rootball and finish with the terminal. The procedure is the same whether the material comes from a nursery can, is dug from the ground, or started from cuttings or seed. Each step in the procedure is detailed as follows:

**Determine root structure.** The position of the surface roots may be a clue to selection of the most attractive side of the bonsai. Remove the rootball from the nursery can or burlap. Brush away the soil that conceals the roots with a small brush, pointed dowel or chopstick. Expose the roots. Be careful to avoid injury to the root surfaces. Do not scrape away their patina. If only sparse roots are apparent, inspect a little deeper for a second layer of rootage. You also will find better trunk taper as you probe lower into the rootball. If heavier roots are not available, work with the ones you have. Prune away any surplus growth arising as multiple trunks if these additional trunks are not needed in the styling. Prune away roots that encircle the base or coil over other roots.

The form and structure of the roots are just as essential as the artistry of the top. They are the most important requisite in creating the image of age. (See sections on *Root Styling*, page 32 and *Handling the Rootball*, page 36.)

Next, wrap the rootball in newspaper and moisten the wrapping to help prevent root dehydration. Then tie the specimen to a turntable or lazy susan. If you expect to work on more bonsai, inexpensive plastic turntables can be purchased at the kitchenware sections of most variety stores. The rootball also can be tied to an inverted flower pot to secure the planting while you are working on it. Your attention now will be devoted to handling the top after which you will return to the rootball for root styling and the potting procedure.

**Establish the front view.** The "front" of the bonsai is the all-important part of the tree which highlights the most attractive features. Evaluate each of the major factors (roots, trunk, branches, foliage) as described in "Order of Importance," page 15). There is no "front" of a tree growing in nature, so artistic taste and ease of styling with the available components are the criteria.

The front usually will be determined by an attractive trunk shape, by choosing the thickest part to be in full view, by looking for curved, gnarled or gracefully twisted branches. The front also can be selected by location of the main branches which should originate from the side of the trunk rather than from the front or back. Position of the surface roots are also a determining factor. Some-times viewing the trunk at different angles to change the position and then rotating the tree will supply a clue. Sometimes there is no option, so we must select as the "front" the view of the tree with the most positive features and the fewest negative ones in a considered compromise.

**Determine the style.** The Japanese have skillfully established the basic bonsai styles depending on the slant of the trunk. Sometimes the style, as analyzed from the material at hand, is quite obvious. These fortunate situations occur when the material obviously must be shaped into a cascade or semi-cascade style because of its structure—or a slanting or wind-swept version due to the trunk shape or a dearth of branches on one side. Most often, a decision is not that obvious. Of course, group plantings always are planned in advance. The various rock-planting styles represent extensive projects which require considerable preliminary design and shaping of the rock. More complete details of bonsai shapes and configurations are covered in *The Elements of Bonsai Styles*, page 44).

**Expose the trunk and create a visual line.** The full trunk should be exposed about two-thirds of the way up to create a main line from the very bottom to the top of the terminal. This line will also provide a clue to determine the style. Prune away all growth that interrupts this main line direction.

However, a wisp of a branch lower down and wired slightly to the front of the trunk, but not concealing it completely, will suggest a natural feeling and not disturb the fundamental design. Make a "see through" effect. The trunk may be interrupted with a jinned terminal, but it should never end with a truncated, pruned appearance. If this is inevitable, conceal the area with foliage passing along the front and top (see "The Terminal Problem," page 24). Nothing can be done with a thick, unbendable trunk by way of shaping except to wait for nature to age it. With junipers and other coniferous species, jin and shari (see page 38) can be created to enhance the aging appearance. Of course, the bark should never be girdled around the trunk. This can be fatal.

**Select and wire the branches.** Wiring bonsai has been called a "ritual" because it appears to be a never-ending occupation. While branches must be wired for shaping from the very beginning, the reward comes when the shapes become fixed and the wire can be removed. Only then can we realize that love's labor is not lost. (For wiring technique, see *The Wiring Ritual*, page 77).

Branches and trunks must be wired to provide interesting curves, to shorten a monotonous straight branch by curving it, to accentuate "ideal," to accent "picturesque," to depict "age" and to conceal "faults." Wiring is the main contrast between a bonsai and a "tree-in-a-pot." Wiring represents the paint and colors of the artist, the sculpture chipping away the stone to expose the image. Wiring is the tool of bonsai creation. It requires only a little practice to master the skill and, after that, it goes fast. The results are apparent immediately. The Japanese masters never observe wire when viewing bonsai; they see only the shapes the wire intended.

The position of the first or lowest branch on the trunk usually will determine the height of the finished bonsai. The distance from the soil line to the first branch should represent, ideally, approximately one-third the height of the tree. This branch should be the thickest and longest but not thicker than the trunk where it emerges, and it could be situated either on the right side or the left side of the trunk. This is identified as the No. 1 branch (see Photo #7).

Prune other thick branches away and work only with thin and medium branches for the rest. The contrast between trunk and thin branches makes the trunk appear thicker by comparison.

On the opposite side of the trunk and above the No. 1 branch—and also a little thinner than No. 1—position branch No. 2. If the finished bonsai will be short, not over twelve inches tall, the distance between the branches No. 1 and No. 2 will be about three or four inches. If the finished tree is to be taller, the distance between these branches will be longer. These main branches should ultimately be wired to reach toward the front and center as if to embrace the viewer. They should never be so close together that they look as if they are directly opposite each other (bar branches).

Branches toward the top should be thinner and convey the impression of newness. They should be wired so they gradually extend in an upward position. Spaces between branches below should be wider than spaces at the top. Lower branches should be wired downward, tips pointing upward.

The back branch is designated as No. 3 and, ideally, should be situated *between* branches No. 1 and No. 2. The back branch can also be positioned above branches No. 1 and No. 2 if there is no other choice. The worst location, except in an emergency, is at the same level or below No. 1.

**Back branch syndrome.** Many bonsai novices worry and fret about a back branch and often pick a poor styling rather than compromise. The purpose of the back branch (or branch No. 3) is to provide depth to the styling. The important thing is that foliage should be apparent at the back when viewed from the front. This can be accomplished by having a single branch growing from the back of the trunk and visible from the front (the classic way), or you can have a "clutch" of branches growing in that location. The illusion of a back branch can also be represented by wiring a side branch so one or more of the twigs looks as if it is

growing from the back of the trunk. Don't worry if the back branch is only a wisp in the beginning. After a season or two, it will fulfill the purpose.

Paradoxically, the back branch should not point directly "backward," but slightly to the right of the trunk or slightly to the left of it so it is not totally obstructed by the trunk when viewed from the front. The thickness of the back branch is not critical. The foliage is what counts.

After the major branches have been selected, remove the unwanted branches—those that are too thick or too thin, out of position, damaged or otherwise not useful to the design. Usually, the medium-thick branches are the most desirable. If a branch is located in an awkward location or otherwise dispensable but fully visible from the front, it can be de-barked and jinned (converted to driftwood) for an additional artistic touch.

Three branches, prudently arranged, are the minimum required for a bonsai. If you are blessed with material that provides generous branching opportunities, the selection of branch Nos. 1, 2 and 3 will be relatively easy and the same sequence of 1-2-3 should be continued up the trunk in layers to the very top. Remember, the branches should be thinner and spaced closer together as they grow upward. Ideally, the pattern should be such that branches emerge from the trunk in different positions to avoid one branch growing directly over another. They should be staggered like spokes in a wheel when viewed from the top.

No branches should grow from the front of the trunk except at the very top which should taper into a recognizable, realistic apex or crown.

**The terminal problem.** As mentioned previously, the height of the bonsai is determined by the position of the first branch, or branch No. 1. This should be ideally positioned at about one-third the tree height. The rest of the tree to the terminal, therefore, should represent about two-thirds the total height. The tree height can also be estimated at about six times the trunk diameter at the base, but an easier rule-of-thumb is the position of the first branch. The terminal then becomes an important factor for estimating the tree height.

Collected material and well-established nursery stock often present a styling problem in the development of a distinct terminal. Nature creates terminals by extending the trunk from the growing tip and the result is a gradual taper from the base to the apex. If the terminal is damaged or broken off by a natural disaster, the closest branch takes over and continues the top growth. Of course, the change in direction is altered due to the bend in the trunk, but the substitute branch functions as the original terminal once did, even if it is visually flawed.

Handling the terminal in bonsai often presents one of the most disturbing problems in design and a poorly

PHOTO #7
Japanese yew, Taxus cuspidata,
23-inches tall, potted 1974 from nursery stock.

*The portion of the trunk below the first branch, for ideal styling, should represent approximately one-third of the tree height. In the specimen pictured, the first branch is somewhat higher than ideal. The jin and shari, however, and other weatherbeaten features compensate for the flawed position of the No. 1 branch. The effect could have been improved by wiring this branch downward to fill in the open space with foliage.*

constructed terminal can be one of bonsai's glaring faults. We want unswerving fidelity to nature—as perfect a terminal as possible. A problem terminal often occurs when the bonsai, in process of styling, is too tall.

The usual procedure, to reduce the tree height to size, is to lop off the trunk somewhere near a suitable branch in the terminal area. The branch then is wired in the same direction as the trunk to create a surrogate terminal. If the continued branch is the same thickness as the truncated portion and if the branch grows from the front so the pruning cut could be made at the back and be concealed, then there is no problem; the continuation in a few growing seasons will be completely obscured.

Seldom, however, do we achieve this ideal (see Photo Sequence #8). More often than not, the branch forming the new terminal continuation is too narrow in contrast to the existing trunk. If a side branch is wired in place for the terminal extension rather than a front branch, the deception will be even more obvious. This seldom looks realistic no matter how skillfully the bend matches the straightness of the trunk at the very top. The surrogate terminal is always there to remind the viewer that the trunk was amputated.

It is possible to conceal the disfigurement with foliage wired in place to hide the fault until time has taken over to fatten the reconstruction. Also, the new terminal will expand in thickness much faster to match the original trunk if branchlets sprouting from it are allowed to grow wild.

Frequently, in these situations, the trunk terminal is not shortened all the way. The truncated portion is kept longer by four or five inches or more to extend the top as a continuation of the trunk. A few branches are retained to create realism. Then the whole top is jinned (see page 38) including a few, thin residual branches to represent a logical apex (see Photo Sequence #1). At least the suggestion is there that a terminal did exist at one time even if the terminal, after jinning and bleaching, appears to have been struck by lightning. As a final alteration, a live branch wired upward adjacent to the jinned terminal, while not in perfect alignment, has a reason to be there, too.

A more drastic operation is to carve away a section of the lopped-off terminal to create better taper and apex. This surgery never produces a natural look, however, and often creates an unattractive scar. If the carved portion accidently encircles the bark, the portion above it will die.

A third option is to style the tree in the informal upright or slanting style so the terminal appears to be curved naturally over the base—a solution where a simple change of direction masks the alteration (see Photo Sequence #1).

**The final terminal solution.** Another way to style the top is to qualify the rule that every bonsai must have a distinct terminal. If you are disturbed because it seems impossible to create a realistic terminal in your styling plan, create a crown. This will consist of several branches growing as a continuation of the trunk and rounded off to represent the top of the tree. Except for the conifers, many species grow without an extension of the trunk pointing upward. Elms grow naturally in a goblet-shaped broom style; maple dissectum varieties grow naturally with several terminals in the shape of a crown. Gnarled apples have the same appearance, often developing two or three trunk extensions at the top, rounding off gracefully. (See Photos #9 and #10).

Perhaps the only solution to "terminal dilemma" is to steer clear of large field grown material that must be severely reduced in height. It is better to select shorter specimens where continuity between the trunk and reconstructed terminal can be more realistic.

In summary, the whole idea is to finish off the top without a noticeable difference in trunk taper. This can be accomplished as follows: (1) form a distinct apex with a suitable branch, (2) create a jin where appropriate, (3) style the top with a pleasing crown.

### STYLING SPECIFICS AND DESIGN FAULTS

Bonsai are not graded from fair to poor to excellent. There is no such thing as a "good" bonsai. Which is better a Rembrandt or a van Gogh? The criterion is the mental image it evokes in the eye of the observer. Does it look like an ideal and picturesque tree in nature? If so, it has delivered the promise. Does it resemble a forest in the wilderness? If *yes*, the styling is successful. If it falls somewhat short of the goal, it still can be a great source of pleasure. Bonsai masterpieces are few and far between. Once the skills are mastered, art enters the picture. Time is, by far, the greatest contribution to a creditable bonsai.

Suggestions that contribute to "ideal" and "picturesque" bonsai are discussed in "The Bonsai Mystique," pages 11–14. The technique for creating faultless bonsai, however, can no more be documented with an instruction sheet than asking an architect how to design a building or an artist how to paint a picture. In bonsai, we want style elements that communicate a feeling of "picturesque." And we eliminate growth features that contradict "ideal."

1. Avoid a branch growing from a concave curve in the trunk. Try to select branches that grow from convex curves. (See Photo #11). Also, too many curves in a trunk become tiresome, like a fanciful curlicue. Two or three curves in the trunk, with attending branches, is about the maximum for good taste.

2. Look for material with a distinct taper from bottom to top. A straight trunk is uninteresting, except for the bunjin style. Likewise, a taper too severe, as we

(CONTINUED ON PAGE 31)

PHOTO SEQUENCE #8
Chinese elm, Ulmus parviflora,
14-inches tall, potted 1980 from nursery stock.

*The desire for plant stock with thick trunks becomes irresistible among growers who graduated from pencil-thin nursery material. The styling technique to reconstruct the terminal, however, may lead to disappointment. Pictured here is an example of a terminal problem that never was fully solved ("Before").*

*The usual procedure is to train a branch growing upward, preferably one growing from the front of the trunk to conceal the pruning scar. Then the branch is wired in place to continue upward growth. This technique, indeed, does provide the tree with a new apex. More often than not, the terminal looks artificial especially if the thickness of the old trunk and the new terminal do not match. Unless a branch similar in caliper to the truncated portion is available, the alteration will seldom look realistic.*

*There are other ways to handle the terminal when we have to deal with this problem. The top can be styled with a crown to neutralize the pruned top rather than attempt to establish a new terminal. Also, this elm could have been converted to a broom style which is a more natural style for elm and zelkova species. Several seasons of growth would be required for conversion to the broom style, but a more creditable bonsai might have been the result.*

*The terminal was reduced in height. Lower branches were thinned and wired downward ("After"). No attempt was made to conceal the unfortunate terminal extension because it is too long. Even at this stage, the plant would have been a good candidate for a "broom." The plant could have been restyled by sacrificing the long, thin trunk and lateral branches. New growth at the truncated portion would develop upward for conventional broom configuration. Several seasons of growth would be required for this conversion.*

BEFORE

AFTER

PHOTO #9
Flowering crabapple, Malus sp.,
22-inches tall, potted 1982 from collected material.

*This collected crabapple with strong surface roots and thick trunk (four inches wide at the base) must have been thoroughly browsed by deer or cattle to have retained such a thick and prominent right-hand branch. While the heaviest branch classically should be No. 1, collected specimens cannot always be styled according to orthodox standards. Their beauty lies in the wild and rugged feeling they convey. Powerful, beautifully-shaped branches should be worked into the design rather than sacrificed to accommodate design standards.*

*Typical of collected specimens that lack definite terminals, this tree was styled with a crown. Apples in nature grow with a central canopy of foliage rather than a single trunk extension. Young apples, under ten years old, develop with a central extension that serves as a terminal. Photo at right shows the bonsai after autumn defoliation.*

*This bonsai was allowed to develop long branches for several growing seasons in order to thicken them and create more picturesque configuration through the "grow and clip" method of shaping. Since apple branches are exceptionally brittle and those in this specimen are rather critical, wiring was dispensed with entirely.*

*A container was selected with a simple shape to enhance contrast with the rugged plant elements.*

PHOTO #10
Birdsnest spruce, Picea abies 'Nidiformis,'
22-inches tall, potted 1982 from nursery stock.

*While branching is sparse on the left side of the tree, asymmetrical balance was accomplished by the heavy branching on the right. Balance was further enchanced by slanting the tree to the left. A portion of the back branch was wired to the left to fill in an empty space resulting from the branch that died. This branch was jinned, but adjacent growth has concealed it.*

*Jinned branches must always be fully exposed and visible. Since thick, dead branches are impossible to shape with wire, the branch was cut halfway through close to the trunk and bent downward. The severed opening was filled with epoxy packing.*

*The trunk was carved for shari, but has become overgrown with callus which makes the shari less apparent. The callus edges could be scraped away to expose the heartwood again and bleached to enhance the effect.*

*While the container could be an inch or two wider for better proportion with the tall tree, the pot depth compensates to add visual bottom weight to the styling.*

PHOTO #11
Hinoki cypress, Chamaecyparis obtusa 'Hinoki,'
15-½ inches tall, potted 1979 from nursery stock.

*A strong branch growing from a convex curve creates asymmetrical balance with the left side of the trunk. Two curves in the trunk with the terminal over the base are typical of informal upright styling. The lowest and heaviest branch extends over the widest portion of the container.*

sometimes see in bald cypress, is exaggerated and not realistic to our observations from nature. Discreetly curved trunks and branching from outside curves are ideal.

3. Triangulation in the silhouette, either in the vertical dimension or the horizontal, should be planned during branch pruning. Triangulation has a symbolic meaning to the Japanese (heaven, earth, humanity). Shortening some branches and leaving others longer will accomplish this.

4. Except in the formal upright style, vary the branch lengths on right and left to balance the proportion. Slant the trunk so the heavy branches on one side compensate for lighter ones on the other side.

5. Avoid opposite branches on a single trunk, twin trunk or two-tree plantings. Prune away branches that create this appearance, except a back branch that grows from the same position on the trunk as a side branch. When viewed from the front, the back branch will not appear to be at the same level.

6. Parallel branches, while appearing in nature, are uninteresting. Simply wire them apart to grow in different planes.

7. Avoid branches terminating in a U, branches growing straight up or straight down. Remove offending branches or wire them straight out, starting with a slight curve upward from the trunk followed by a graceful downward curve. Branch ends should point upward.

8. Branch shapes should be the same on both sides of the tree, lower branches shaped downward, upper branches curved upward. No branch should point straight out in the front except at the very terminal and, then, very short like new growth.

9. Avoid branches that cross. Alter their positions with wire or remove one offender. Branches below should be thicker than those above wherever possible. A thick branch in the terminal area is taboo because it is unreal. Remove branches growing straight up or inward.

10. Clean away foliage growth underneath a branch so the branch line is readily apparent from the front. Ideally, branches should be trimmed in the same triangular shape as the silhouette when viewed from the top. Each branch should end with a distinct terminal. Remove growth from crotches unless a new branch is desired in that position.

## PREPARING THE ROOTBALL FOR POTTING

The top of the tree has been styled, the branches wired, the all-important front has been selected, the style has been determined. The next function concerns the roots and rootball and getting it into the pot.

Nurserymen tell us that material grown in cans or supplied balled and bagged becomes rootbound with roots radiating around the rootball. This makes it all but impossible for new roots to reach out of the compact mass and into the surrounding soil. The recommendation: Loosen the soil to free the roots before planting in the garden. The same holds true when potting such material into a pot for bonsai. *Roots should be combed out to allow them to grow into new soil.* This also applies to re-potting.

The potbound situation that occurs in the nursery is known as a "coil." Removal of this coil is one of the most important steps in transplanting such stock into a bonsai pot. The roots must be freed from the ball, sometimes with considerable effort, uncoiled and cut back. Otherwise, the roots may just continue to grow 'round and 'round. Coiled roots on the soil surface are unattractive.

Nurserymen also have discovered that mere "spading" of the rootball smooths and compresses the adjacent soil surface preventing fine root hairs from penetrating the barrier. Do everything possible to make it easy for roots to come through into new soil when potting commercial nursery material.

**Root functions.** The purpose of feeder roots is to transport moisture and nourishment to the plant above. Taproots serve seedlings only. They can be severed completely without harm to the system. Taproots can be identified as long, tapered roots going straight down, or almost straight down, with no fibrous growth at the ends. When a seed drops to the ground, a tiny living thread inside is forced to point downward by gravity. When the seed bursts open due to moisture, this thread becomes a taproot which quickly grows into the soil to provide moisture and nutrition for the seedling until fibrous roots can take over. While the taproot continues to grow in nature to stabilize the plant until other roots mature, its function is that of a stabilizer rather than a pipeline.

**Root pruning proportion.** The first potting requires extensive root pruning as the first stage to miniaturization and the top must be pruned in proportion. When roots are reduced in greater proportion to the top, branches and foliage may die back due to functional stress. The roots have lost the full capacity to supply the top with moisture.

When the top is reduced in greater proportion to the roots, the reverse occurs; foliage growth becomes very active while the surplus and unneeded roots go dormant and eventually disappear.

The pruning formula for the first potting is this: If one-third of the roots are pruned away, half the top can be sacrificed without creating an imbalance. Tackle the old growth first.

**Root pruning technique.** When exposing roots from the rootball, loosen the soil with a chopstick or root tool. Work gently. Spray the root mass frequently. Tease the roots out carefully. Do not work in the sun or a draft. Ideally, the roots should be distributed evenly around the trunk. No roots should point straight forward. Take care not to scrape the root surfaces. The roots develop in a tubelike structure and once the patina is punctured, the tube cannot function. Getting the roots out of the ball and functionable in a pot is probably the most critical operation in the transformation.

Comb the soil from the roots in the direction they are growing, first from the sides and then from the bottom. If roots are badly intertwined, separate them gently so they hang out of the ball. Prune out, first, the largest roots without fibrous root ends that only take up soil space.

Always keep new root growth when you have a choice. New growth is more active and develops faster. It can be identified as the soft, white tip at the end of the root terminal which starts as a single cell and expands as it extends. Even if the root is a foot long, only the white, fibrous end does the work of sustaining the top. Trimming a portion of these root ends stimulates new fibrous growth just as trimming branch ends stimulates foliage. That is why re-potting revitalizes the root system.

**Managing a compacted rootball.** Sometimes the rootball is so compacted, prying with a chopstick or a root tool is insufficient to separate the root mass. Mutilating the rootball can seriously damage the root system and retard development. In such situations, it is better to risk bare-root potting. Soak the ball in a tub of water. Then hose the soil to wash it away for easier root pruning.

Finally, allow the trimmed root mass to protrude from the soil ball about an inch to come in contact with new soil. In addition, keep some untrimmed roots to enter the new soil to provide a lifeline until the rest of the system is restored. Select the newest growth with vigorous ends to keep untrimmed.

**Surface roots.** While loosening the rootball, watch out for surface roots you want to retain. In nature, the large surface roots with fibrous roots at the end of them, provide ballast; in bonsai, the flared, buttressed surface roots are an integral part of the design. Avoid damaging these surface roots and keep them long enough to function.

ROOT STYLING

Strong surface roots are the most important requisite to communicate an image of age in bonsai. While many old trees do lack conspicuous roots above ground, this lack of surface roots generally is associated with immature trees and saplings. Just as branches need selection when bonsai are styled, so attention should also be given to root design and detailing if choices are available.

1. Avoid surface roots that cross over other roots. They should be separated or one or the other should eventually be removed.

2. If a root curves above the soil line, tie the root in place with string during potting. The string will decompose and the root will remain where it belongs. Another option is to remove a wedge from the root to straighten it out. The root either will continue to function or throw out new rootlets where severed. It will remain in position until self-repair occurs.

3. If surface roots are lacking on one side of the trunk, a strategically placed rock positioned as an outcropping will fill in optically where the surface root is desired. The rock should be inconspicuous and blend in with the color of existing roots—below the soil surface rather than setting on top of the soil (see Photo Sequence #12). Or the front of the tree can be arranged so the side lacking roots is close to the pot edge which will make the bare side less apparent.

4. Good grooming suggests that root hairs exposed on the soil surface should be clipped off. They perform no function when dried and they spoil the surface-root appearance.

5. If an otherwise satisfactory trunk lacks strong surface roots, don't despair. Even small roots supply a hint of what should be there. Sometimes it is possible to bare more of the lower trunk to expose better roots. If more roots are still absent, you may end up with a better trunk taper at the surface.

6. An unwanted root too high on the trunk should be inspected before it is removed. There may be vital fibrous roots at the end of it which could represent the tree's lifeline. If there are strong root masses in other sections of the rootball, this root can be sacrificed. If not, wind this long root around the rootball to preserve the fibrous ends until new fibrous roots can develop closer to the trunk elsewhere in the rootball. At the next potting time, the long root can be shortened. Some fibrous roots must always be present at potting even if they are temporarily out of place.

7. Surface roots should not lay on the soil as if they were placed there like sticks on the ground. They should be partially planted as if the soil eroded from the roots to expose them.

8. Trident maple "tunnels": The buttressed root formation of trident maples often results in tunnel-like openings which can be disturbing. While trident maple roots have the capacity to self-graft, which means that an opening may disappear in time, it will take years before this takes effect. Again, an inconspicuous rock

PHOTO #12
Juniper Shimpaku, Juniperus chinensis var. Sargentii,
18-inches tall, potted 1979 from nursery stock.

*While the trunk in this specimen shows satisfactory taper and buttressing, surface roots are lacking on the right side which presents an unstable appearance ("Before" photo). One solution could have been to slant the trunk downward so the barren side is closer to the soil surface. Then the trunk could have been wired so eye movement runs from left to right with a terminal wired directly over the base for additional balance. The roots on the left side then would appear to stabilize the slanted direction.*

*An alternate design option ("After" photo) was selected through placement of an inconspicuous rock to fill in optically where surface roots are desired. The rock should blend in color with existing roots rather than constitute an "attention getter." The rock is buried partially into the soil to represent a natural outcropping.*

BEFORE                                   AFTER

approximately the same color as the trunk can be fitted into the opening to conceal it if the opening faces the viewer. Or the tree can be potted so the opening is not as apparent from the front of the planting. A heavily buttressed trunk, a characteristic of the trident maple, is a most desirable feature but an unwanted opening at the base may be disturbing.

### PREPARING THE POT

The roots have been pruned and new growth extends from the rootball for penetration into new soil. The soil has been mixed and ready for use (see "Soils," page 51). Once, again, moisten the rootball, wrap it with newspaper and tie it with string to guard against dehydration.

**Rootball anchorage.**  Fasten plastic screen squares over the drainage holes with clips fashioned from copper wire. Thread one or more anchor wires through the holes from the bottom of the pot, through the screens and long enough to encircle the ball. For pots with a single drainage hole, twist the wires around a nail or piece of heavy wire to secure the anchor on the outside bottom of the pot. These wires will be inserted through the rootball and twisted together so the rootball stays anchored.

While it is best to secure rootballs in some way, large rootballs need not be anchored if there are ample roots and soil to serve as ballast. If the ball moves around in the pot due to inadquate anchorage or root mass to hold the ball in place, tie it up with string from the outside or inside instead of wire. After a few months, new roots will take hold and the string can be removed. Do not use nylon or plastic string inside the pot as it will not decompose. Trees that wobble in a pot will take a long time to get settled. Even slight movement caused by breezes can keep fine root hairs from becoming established.

Orientation of plant and pot is the next stage in the potting procedure.

### POTTING POSITION AND PLACEMENT

There is no reason why a potential bonsai acquired as nursery stock or collected from nature has to be potted as it grew in the can or wild in the woodland. Orientation in the bonsai *pot* involves another artistic consideration. It is much more than merely making sure the front of the tree is where it belongs. (See Photo Sequence #13).

It is too late to make major changes once the ball is wired into place and final soil added, unless the dry soil is dumped out and you start over again. Even then, the risk is considerable. Minor adjustments in position can be made, however, if the wire is not yet fully tightened.

**The artistic approach.**  There is invariably one best possible position. Take the time to figure it out. Place the plant into the empty pot to get a good view of all the elements. Slowly rotate the trunk. Carefully observe the plant from all angles—front to back, left to right, trunk angulation. Do the surface roots splay out correctly? Does the root in front point out at the viewer? Surface roots should be evenly distributed around the base and, ideally, none should point out toward the front. Very often, the plant can be turned slightly to avoid this. The surface roots, also, should be partially buried as if exposed by soil erosion. A thick surface root that bends or arches can be straightened by wiring a splint underneath the root. Protect the upper surface with rubber to keep the wire from cutting in.

Look at the plant as an architect studies a preliminary design. Is the terminal sufficiently wired toward the viewer—or too much? Shift and turn the plant to bring into full view the most attractive branch and trunk shapes. A slight change may dramatically improve the picture. Some slight wiring adjustments may have to be made at this time and it's better now than later. So often there is a feeling of "position regret" after a potentially classic bonsai has been potted and slight corrections that could have been made were overlooked.

**Observe the curves.**  The first curve of the trunk at the base should slant away from the viewer if you have a choice. On the other hand, the whole top portion of the tree, about one-third, should curve slightly *toward* the viewer. If it curves away, straighten it with wire before potting. If it is too thick to bend and straighten, conceal the backward curve with a little foliage and exaggerate the terminal bend toward the viewer. The terminal is invariably thin and supple and easy to bend.

**Bonsai styles suggest potting positions.**  Informal upright and slanting styles should be potted in rectangular or oval containers, off center and very slightly to the rear. The lowest branch or the longest branch should extend over the widest soil area. This generally is branch No. 1.

Formal upright plantings are centered in the pot, slightly to the rear. Bonsai potted in round or square containers also are centered. Avoid round or square pots for plantings that suggest off-center positioning.

**Visual movement.**  Plant orientation in the pot also is determined optically by the sense of direction as evidenced by the shape of the trunk, branches and terminal, as follows:

1. If direction is to the left, position the tree to the right so the eye moves toward the widest area of soil. (See Photo Sequence #14). If direction is to the right, reverse the position.    (CONTINUED ON PAGE 36)

## PHOTO SEQUENCE #13
Maple dissectum, Acer palmatum dissectum atro-purpureum rubrum,
28-inches tall, potted 1971 from field-grown stock.

*This bonsai originally was potted with the long branch extended over the widest soil area which positioned the tree to the extreme right ("Before"). When the branches were trimmed and the tree re-potted, the pot was positioned under the foliage ("After") which shifted the trunk to a more pleasing location. The contrast in appearance is obvious.*

*Note, also, that the left side shows evidence of long internodes and sparse foliage compared to the right side. This is the direct result of unequal sun exposure. Branches on the right side received more light than those on the left.*

*While maple dissectum varieties should be displayed in partial shade from the latter part of July to the end of August, it also is important that all sides receive uniform light. Several hours each day, however, the left side of this tree was shaded by a large oak. Several seasons in the same location compounded the problem which suggests, again, that bonsai should be rotated weekly for uniform sun exposure on all sides.*

**BEFORE**

**AFTER**

2. For a styling showing a long curve of the trunk with a terminal directly over the base, center the pot under the *foliage*. Do not use the trunk as the criterion for positioning which may shift the plant to an extreme location on the right or left. Sometimes a slight tilt will change an ordinary appearance to an interesting one of unsymmetrical balance (See Photo #10).

Finally, realize that the eye is the best judge of esthetics and that is what positioning and orientation are all about. Always balance the tree in the pot so it looks comfortable. If branches were wired with an original concept in mind, the branch positions may have to be adjusted when the tree is finally prepared for the pot. You may find that what you thought was a branch suitably wired parallel to the soil surface now becomes a branch pointing upward. The branch positions were changed because you tilted the trunk. Sometimes branches will have to be re-wired in the interest of orientation if they cannot be adjusted by bending.

POTTING THE ROOTBALL

You are now ready for the final operation in the sequence. The plant has been styled, the roots were trimmed, the ball reduced in size to fit into the pot with an inch or two of fresh soil for the roots to enter; the pot has been prepared with wire, the holes covered with screens and, finally, you have decided on the perfect orientation for the marriage of tree to pot.

**Fixing position.**    Remove the moistened newspaper from around the ball and spray once more. With a small scoop, place about an inch of soil on the bottom of the pot for pots up to two-inches deep. For deeper pots, increase the first layer of soil accordingly. Now place the rootball on this bottom soil layer and gently rotate the ball to the right and left as if to screw the ball into the pot. Make sure all exposed roots contact fresh soil. If position adjustments are necessary, add a little soil beneath the ball on one side to change the angle—or pull a little soil away on the other side to lower the ball. Orientation at this stage is critical.

Now you are ready to wire the ball in place. With a gimlet or knitting needle, make a hole in the ball so the wire, already prepared, will travel straight through without bending if it contacts a solid root. Then insert one end of the wire through this hole and twist it to the other end of the wire. With a pliers, bend the two ends together. Hold your hand over the rootball and pull the twisted wires toward you, at the same time twisting the wire ends together until the ball is totally secure. Of course, the wire should not be twisted so much that the roots are damaged. Just tighten enough so the ball is steady. Clip off the unused wire and push the severed ends into the soil and out of the way.

**Adding final soil.**    Once the rootball is secure and you are satisfied with the final position the plant will occupy in the pot, add more soil to fill the pot. Use a chopstick or pointed dowel to settle the soil around the roots. Do not attack the soil mass with a jabbing or stabbing motion. Insert the chopstick and rotate it until the soil disappears into the air pockets. Repeat the process until all air pockets and spaces have been eliminated. If the pot is large, pound each side of the pot with your fist several times. Finally, in order to settle the soil thoroughly around the root ends, lift the pot off the table about an inch and tap the pot lightly to the table top two or three times.

Remember, all operations involving the soil and rootball must be handled gently. Scooping the soil into the pot, distributing the soil around exposed root hairs, settling the soil with a chopstick and tapping the pot on the table top—all can brutalize the roots and cause stress. Roots are tough. They can take some rough treatment in the course of potting, but it makes sense to handle carefully.

**Mounded potting.**    The root ball should be mounded slightly so it slopes gradually from the trunk to the pot edge. (See Photo Sequence #3). The trunk should never be positioned in a depression. In addition to mounding slightly, the soil should slope to the pot edge about one-quarter inch below the pot rim so the soil surface can accumulate water to percolate to the soil below and not run off and drain away. If the root ball is mounded at too steep an angle, it is bound to erode and fill the space you set aside for water. As the erosion develops, remove the soil from around the pot edge to restore a watering space.

**Preserving bark.**    Do not touch bark excrescences on the trunk with your hands when working on the tree. Rough bark will last a long time if not removed mechanically, although it may not be possible to avoid disturbing some furrowed bark when applying wire to a branch that also involves the trunk. When lifting out of a pot a tree with attractive bark, hold the tree at the very top rather than low down at the base. Bark at the top usually is young and smooth and will not be damaged when grasped.

**Mycorrhizae—how it works.**    If you encounter a whitish, stringy fungus in the soil during potting, preserve it. This is mycorrhizal fungi, the beneficial organisms that thrive on the roots of pines and other species, send strands into the surrounding soil and which act as an extended root system to the host. This extension of the roots through the mycorrhizae fungi greatly increases the uptake of moisture and nutrients. It often can be found clinging to the inside of the container and

## PHOTO SEQUENCE #14
Juniper Shimpaku, Juniperus chinensis var. Sargentii,
22-inches tall, potted 1978 from nursery stock.

*Constant nipping and pinching while the branch terminal buds are soft produces the cloud-like growth response ("Before"). While the rich foliage conceals the branching fretwork and ramification, the dominant foliage is one of several options available in styling this juniper variety. Drastic pruning could have outlined the branching pattern, but the cloud-like silhouette tends to conceal an otherwise uninteresting straight trunk.*

*As a result of the gradual training through pinching the branch ends, scale-like or whipcord growth has been retained. Juvenile growth, characterized by needle-like foliage, invariably results from over-pruning Shimpaku juniper. The pinching thus provides a gradual transformation in contrast to what may have resulted through drastic use of the pruning shears. The foliage is thinned out moderately each autumn to allow light and air to penetrate ("After"). The planting is kept in full sun.*

*Eye movement of this bonsai is right to left and the tree is potted off-center. Since the terminal has a tendency to drift upward, it is wired each spring to re-establish its position directly over the base for typical informal upright styling.*

*The position of the strong roots on the right side counter-balances the weight on the left. Because of the trunk slant, a portion of surface roots were concealed below the soil on the left side—an unfortunate compromise when the trunk angle is so altered.*

**BEFORE**

**AFTER**

it should be left in place if the same pot is to be used in repotting. One caution, however: When you spray for fungi on species other than pine, keep the spray away from the pine species. The fungicide will also destroy the fungi you want to retain.

**Potting aids.**   An effective tool for prying roots clear of the rootball is a "baling hook" which can be purchased at most hardware stores. This is a strong, hook-like tool fixed into a comfortable handle. One of the best tools to use for trimming fine roots combed out of the rootball is an ordinary household scissors. It cuts cleanly and fast. Also, an old toenail clipper (the style shaped like a pliers) is ideal for getting in and around hard-to-reach places. And a handy device to smooth soil surface after potting is a one-inch wide, long-bristled paint brush with the bristles cut at a 45° angle. The pointed end makes it easy to get around the trunk without disturbing the soil. Just clip away the unwanted portion of the bristles with a heavy scissors at the desired angle.

### JIN, SHARI AND URO

In Japanese terminology, "jin" is a dead tip on a trunk or branch that has been worked into the styling, or an entire branch can be so designed. The bark is scraped off to heartwood. "Shari" is the same treatment of the trunk where an area of bark has been peeled back to expose heartwood. Care must be taken to avoid girdling. The idea is to give bonsai the appearance of a natural catastrophe as if the branch or trunk were struck by lightning. "Uro" is a hollowed-out trunk or split trunk and also conveys a lightning-struck result that has been weathered by wind and sun. (See Photo #15).

When creating jin, the branch must be trained with wire and bent immediately after the bark has been removed. Once the branch dies, it will be impossible to shape.

Jin should always be located in the front of healthy foliage and should not cross live branches nor be concealed by live branches—and it should be positioned somewhat to the right or left of the trunk rather than centered. The dead wood should stand out as a separate element. The angle and direction of jinned branches must correspond with the configuration of existing branches. The effect should be realistic in appearance rather than an obvious device to attract attention. Indeed, a heavily-jinned bonsai will look artificial.

**What to avoid.**   Do not jin a healthy branch with dense foliage. Likewise, deciduous bonsai are never jinned except for old and gnarled specimens such as apple species. Vigorous growth of most deciduous species soon obscures a jinned portion.

Jinning, however, is especially effective on conifer terminals. When you have a choice of two apexes in a terminal, one should be "jinned" and this should be higher than the true apex. When this is done, part of the trunk should also be exposed as a continuation of the jinned terminal on top. When the bark is peeled off, the exposed portion should taper down the trunk rather than come to an abrupt end. Do not go below the soil surface, but leave a strip of bark about an inch above the soil line to avoid rotting.

Creating jin on back branches is wasted because the effect will not be visible. If a branch in back dies naturally, it is best to amputate it. Reserve the technique for branches that have become weakened through lack of adequate light or damage and that might have had to be amputated anyway. An example of this is the loss of an important branch that originally was included in the styling, but eventually languished. (See Photo Sequence #16).

When single, unimportant branches are considered for jinning, the driftwood effect should be repeated elsewhere on the bonsai to create the illusion that the disaster occurred naturally. Otherwise, a single, thin, unobtrusive branch bared of its bark may look unrealistic.

**Bark peeling for shari.**   Before peeling back the bark of a trunk or partial stripping of a branch, mark the bark to be peeled away with a pointed blade down to the heartwood. In this way, you can control the stripping and you will not exceed the portion to be removed. Peel the bark back with a pliers. To remove bark from a branch, simply squeeze the branch gently with a pliers and pull the bark away with the fingers. Whenever bark is peeled away for jin, remove the cambium layer sheath from the heartwood. Cambium is the live layer between bark and hardwood. Thin-barked and young trees will have to be scraped and sanded.

On a "shari" trunk, callus tissue eventually will develop over the wounded edges and reduce the exposed surface. When this occurs, the callus will have to be cut away to restore the driftwood effect.

**Bleaching dead wood.**   To simulate a weathered effect, jin and shari can be bleached. A striking contrast of driftwood and jinned portions between live branches and foliage can be achieved through the application of a lime-sulphur mixture which can be purchased commercially as Orthorex. This bleaches the dead, woody portions a grayish white. Apply full strength. A small portion of white acrylic water color paint may be added (¼ teaspoon of acrylic to ¼ cup of lime-sulphur solution) plus a few drops of black india ink. The mixture is applied to the wood with a small brush or cotton-tipped applicator during the hottest weather and when the

(CONTINUED ON PAGE 41)

PHOTO #15
Black spruce, Picea mariana,
28-inches tall, potted 1970 from collected material.

*This tree was acquired from an old estate and was estimated to be about fifty years old when potted after two years of training in the ground. Due to the extreme curvature of the trunk and sparse branching, a slanted "windswept" style was chosen. The upper branches were wired windward, but the lower branch was shaped in the reverse direction which sometimes occurs in natural windswept configuration. This also served visually to fill in an open space half-way up the trunk.*

*Borers infested the lower trunk, were eradicated, and the dead wood was carved away for "shari" and "uro." A dead back branch was jinned.*

*The tree developed slowly and it is pinched lightly every other spring in an effort to induce additional branching from the trunk. Old specimens simply do not respond, even after seventeen years in a pot.*

PHOTO SEQUENCE #16
Juniper Shimpaku, Juniperus chinensis var. Sargentii,
19-inches tall, potted 1982 from nursery stock.

*The lower branch gradually declined due to shading from the branches above ("Before"). The branch subsequently was jinned ("After"), thinned and wired with a marked improvement. Note that main branches grow from the outside of trunk curves.*

BEFORE                                    AFTER

jinned portion is very dry. Avoid applying to the live bark and cover the soil with plastic during the procedure. It takes about a week for the bleach to work and it may have to be repeated if the effect is not striking enough. The wood eventually will turn gray with a driftwood appearance.

Finally, jin and shari sometimes can be overdone. The planting becomes a work of art and craft rather than the suggestion of a natural accident. Examples of exaggerated jin can be beautiful beyond description but, often, they appear ostentatious. Jin and driftwood should have a natural affinity to the rest of the styling rather than become the most conspicuous feature.

**Mossing.**  Apply moss to the soil surface piece by piece with the same artistic discretion as the tree is positioned in the pot. (See "Moss and Lichen," page 83.) Never cover the soil completely. Rather, place the moss in patches around the base of the tree. Use moss of different shades of green to vary the effect. Then sift a few pinches of fine soil adjacent to the patches to create an even surface and encourage the moss to fill in the gaps. Lichen is better than moss if you can get it, although lichen does not spread as rapidly. Remember, excessive moss may interfere with drainage and air circulation. At least 75% of the soil surface should be apparent as "soil," not ground cover.

Apply moss so it does not obscure attractive surface-root curves. About half the root diameter should be below the soil and covering the rest of the roots with moss defeats the purpose. Either use moss sparingly adjacent to surface roots or position the root a little higher on the soil surface to compensate for the moss cover.

**Watering.**  The final stage in the potting sequence is watering. Unless the pot is large and cumbersome, the plant should be watered by soaking the pot in a sink or a tub of water. At the same time, spray lightly from above. Allow the pot to soak until air bubbles disappear which usually requires about ten minutes to settle the soil around the roots and disperse air pockets. Keep the water level outside the pot just at the soil level in the pot to avoid disturbing the soil surface and moss.

If the pot and planting are too large to submerge for soaking, water from above with a hose spray or watering can until the soil is thoroughly soaked. When the planting has been thoroughly watered, set it aside and proceed with "After-care."

POTTING AFTER-CARE

"After care" is the opposite of potting *regular care*. For example, newly potted bonsai are kept in shade rather than sun, they are watered infrequently rather than daily, fertilizing should be postponed until new growth is apparent and pruning and pinching is a long way off. The most serious consideration is to help the plant survive from stress and shock and get it on its way and growing.

Saplings from nursery material and young bonsai will recover faster after transplanting—much faster than an older specimen. Nothing can replace the vigor of youth, nor reverse the infirmities of age.

After-care begins by replacing the planting in an area protected from wind and sun which also starts a period of coddling and observation. This also means you will have to "baby" the newly-potted plant until it has become stabilized and the roots have thoroughly recovered from pruning and transplanting shock. How long should this transition period last before bonsai are returned to the display bench? There is no specific timetable. The safety period should continue until signs of permanent, active growth become apparent.

These signs differ with species, age of material, time of potting, amount of root destruction and the season of potting. Conifers will continue to show life signs long after transpiration has been interrupted. Turgidity within the cells is sufficient to keep the branch going for some time. Just observe the lifelike appearance of a newly severed branch from a pine, juniper or taxus. It sometimes takes weeks for a conifer branch to lose the natural, green appearance even when the amputated branch is setting on the ground.

**Recovery period.**  Just because a branch on a bonsai has good color after potting is no reason to assume that vigilance of the after-care period is ended. Active signs of new growth must be apparent. When growth becomes visible, even with the aid of a magnifying glass, it means that roots have resumed activity. Only then is it safe to suspend the period of intensive care. New growth in deciduous species becomes apparent rather quickly—often within a few days after potting, but they also wilt faster than conifer species.

Until moisture transpiration is restored—and there are signs of new growth—a newly potted bonsai should be kept in shade, in an area protected from rain with as much surrounding humidity as possible. This can be accomplished through misting or soaking the ground or bench in the holding area. Simulate "greenhouse" conditions as much as possible.

**Water sparingly.**  When the soil finally dries out, pray that it's not because of dry air but that turgidity has been restored. Apply a small amount of water (an ounce or two at the most) right over the root ball. Since the roots have not yet extended, there is no point in watering the entire soil mass. Continue the intensive care until you observe fresh, new growth all over—not just on a branch or two. You would be surprised if you realized how many bonsai would be alive and prospering were it not for a compromise in the after-care regimen.

Newly potted and root pruned bonsai simply cannot supply moisture to the top until fibrous roots are able to function. Dowsing the soil with water only delays fibrous root recovery and may finish them off. Some newly-potted bonsai will recover quickly and you'll be quick to notice, too. We don't worry about these. It's the slow ones that appear on the border line that require care and caution. When growth-resumption signs are evident, it's time to expose the planting gradually to sunlight starting with dappled light, then half-sun and, finally full sun.

When growth continues for thirty days, it is time to fertilize. Use quarter-strength or half-strength of the quantity indicated on the label. (See "Fertilizing," page 90).

Finally, don't be too quick to pinch back new growth on newly potted material. Let branches elongate. As they do, the roots also extend themselves. Give the tree a chance to respond before you start shaping. Branch ramification is not an overnight proposition.

RE-POTTING

Periodic re-potting of bonsai restores and revitalizes root activity without assuming the risks that drastic root pruning presents at the first potting session. When re-potted at regular intervals, the branches need to be trimmed back only slightly to accommodate the root loss. The branches already had been reduced through pinching and trimming during the growing season. Drastic branch reduction at re-potting time, therefore, is unnecessary. Likewise, roots will require only perfunctory attention when bonsai are re-potted periodically. Combing out and pruning back the long roots so new roots can grow into fresh soil may be all that is required.

**When to repot.** Young bonsai grow faster than older specimens and may require re-potting as often as once a year. Some fast-growing species, such as willows, become potbound in one or two seasons of growth depending on the fertilizing schedule, sunlight and soil drainage. Older bonsai can go years without re-potting, but all bonsai must be re-potted when the root system becomes overgrown.

There are several ways to determine this. First, see if the roots are coming out of the drainage holes. This is a sure sign that re-potting is necessary. Next, sever the wire at the bottom of the pot. Lift out the rootball. If the ball lifts out easily and the roots are not potbound, wait until next season.

If the roots entwine around the pot, however, and they radiate around the rootball like a coil of wire, the roots *are* potbound and re-potting is necessary. In this situation the roots must be reduced more drastically

and more pruning of the top also becomes necessary to compensate for the extensive root loss. The roots and top should be pruned in proportion.

This often presents a problem that may require altering the basic design. If the top is not pruned back in proportion to the severe root loss, the top may die back for lack of roots to supply moisture which means the tree literally will prune itself. That is why it is so important to repot bonsai before the root growth gets out of hand.

**Re-potting alternatives.** One option is to prune overgrown roots moderately as if you had repotted before the crisis. The next season, reduce the roots and top growth even more. This will restore the growth balance.

Another solution is to allow the top growth to become rank. Then severely prune back the unwanted growth after the roots have been trimmed as conservatively as possible. This is almost like starting from scratch.

Also, if a bonsai is not doing well with new, active growth, this may suggest repotting—not because the roots are too copious, but because they may have failed to develop due to poor drainage, or a soil not suitable to the species. In this situation, repot with a soil medium that will get rid of the excess moisture and be compatible with the plant (see "Soils," page 51). When repotting in this situation, the roots need not be pruned at all because root growth may automatically have been retarded due to the inadequate growing medium.

It is not such a big chore to repot regularly. It becomes a project with uncertainty when repotting is neglected.

**Emergency repotting.** If bonsai require repotting at a time unsuitable for the species or the season due to a broken pot, the specimen can be successfully transferred to another pot if the roots are undisturbed and if the procedure merely involves changing the container to one of similar size. Simply transfer the rootball and add whatever new soil is missing.

RESTORING GROUP PLANTINGS

Repotting any bonsai revitalizes the root system and the top responds in proportion. All bonsai, including groups, must be repotted at regular intervals which may vary from annual attention for active species and fast growers to every three to five years for older specimens and slow growers. For group plantings, when you can lift up an edge of the soil in one mass, it is time to repot.

Repotting groups often represents a problem. Separating the various elements and restoring them in the same positions often is frustrating unless a careful chart is drawn in advance showing the exact location of each tree. One method is to lift the entire group from the shallow container, first cutting any wires that anchor the planting to the pot. Then, with a sharp knife, cut away each tree with its own clump of soil and then replace the group, using fresh soil, according to the pre-determined plan. While individual clumps may become a little looser in the soil due to lack of root anchorage, this can be corrected when re-positioned by attaching each clump with new wire glued to the bottom of the pot, by weighting each clump with a rock until the roots take hold again or by applying peat muck to each element to fix it in place below. After a few weeks, the roots, stimulated by pruning, will penetrate the new soil and restore the original stability.

**How to repot groups without taking the plants apart.** This simply involves removing a portion of the soil around the pot edges by cutting it away for an inch or two around the pot perimeter. With a sharp knife, cut away soil, moss and roots. Since each tree in the planting will have sent out roots that circulate around the outside edge of the container, the "coil" encountered represents root overgrowth of each individual tree. Even the roots of those specimens in the center of the container probably will be represented in this "coil." A pot-bound situation in group plantings can thus be avoided simply by reducing the volume of roots represented in the container perimeter.

After the soil and "coils" are removed, add new soil as close in composition to the original as possible. Groups repotted in this manner will continue vigorous, healthy growth in new soil for a long time without having to remove each specimen.

POTTING BRIEFS

During potting, if there is a depression under the root ball, make a mound of soil where the cavity will be. Once the tree is in position, do not move it as this may create an air space. Make all adjustments before watering. Once watered, do not touch the soil. If the soil is pressed after watering, it may compact.

**Pot sizes.** Pot selections are governed by horticultural reasons as well as artistic. Beware the temptation to cut back the roots just to fit the ball into the pot. If the rootball indicates a larger pot than you had in mind, sacrifice the esthetics for safety and postpone the use of a smaller pot until the next potting session.

The preceding potting instructions detail the procedure for the use of conventional bonsai pots. Ideally, there should be about two inches of soil around the outside of the rootball for fibrous roots to explore. Many growers, for reasons of economy, precaution or convenience, choose to avoid the use of ceramic bonsai pots the first time around. Instead, the styled planting is potted in a standard flower pot, an azalea pot which is shallower, a home-made wood container or an inexpensive plastic pot with holes. Clay pots have the advantage of porosity to stimulate aeration of the rootball.

Also, many growers go light on root pruning for the first potting which also demands a larger pot than usual. The roots are pruned a little more drastically at the next potting when the bonsai is finally settled in a suitable bonsai container.

**Changing position.** Sometimes we are displeased with the way a tree sets in a pot after the rootball has been secured with wire and all the soil has been added. If you are tempted to shift a tree by pushing it here and there right after potting, *don't*. This movement will compact the soil and drainage will be ruined. You also will damage many of the fine roots which you were so careful to preserve just a short time before.

**Correcting potting mistakes.** If you are not happy with the position of the tree *after* it has been potted and *before* water and surface moss have been applied, just sever the anchor wire, dump out the soil and start over again. This is the advantage of using soil that is bone dry. If you were cautious in jabbing during the original potting procedure, there will be little damage to the roots. If the rootball has already been watered, it is too late.

**Emergency measure.** When a plant shows signs of decline (sparse new growth, yellowing leaves or needles), remove it from the pot without damaging the roots and shake off as much soil as possible. Do not use a chopstick or other tool. Repot in an oversize container, preferably a standard clay pot, using 100% coarse sand, aquarium sand or chicken grit. Water once and keep the plant shaded. Water again when the sand dries out. When new growth is evident and continuous, repot again in a container larger than the original one and make sure drainage is adequate. Keep in dappled sun.

Another option is to remove the patient from the pot and plant it in a protected area in the ground for a growing season. In both situations, make sure the plant's decline is not the result of an infestation or disease.

**Consequences of potting neglect.** In single plantings, there can be an accumulation of coiled roots inside a rootball hidden by an outer coil. When you trim only the outer coil, the internal coil keeps radiating around. Sometimes these inner coils, resulting from inadequate prior root-prunings, are not even visible without disturbing the root ball.

At repotting time, the root tips must be combed outward from the root ball to penetrate into new soil. Reach in and tease out all the old, concealed, coiled roots to prevent the root mass from becoming choked. When choked, the top starts to decline for no apparent reason. Fast-growing deciduous species such as maples are especially susceptible to this problem.

Sometimes there are several layers of these internally-coiled roots which were repeatedly overlooked at repotting time, concealed by the outer coil. Roots respond to trimming with new growth the same as the top. When roots are trimmed correctly at each repotting session, the repotting regimen can be postponed for three or four years. Bonsai that suffers from a potbound situation caused by excessive coiling will not be revitalized until the internal coils are eliminated. Once they are pruned away and straightened out, the plant responds dramatically.

**Root growth.**   Roots will grow at lower soil temperatures (40°F.) than the tops (about 50°F.). This suggests that repotting in the fall when transpiration and air temperatures are low may be desirable. Bonsai repotted in the fall, however, should never be exposed to freezing temperature. New top growth encouraged by accelerated root activity may be injured. Roots function best at soil temperatures of 65°–80°F. Above 104°F. root tips are killed.

**Screen nightmare.**   One of the worst things that can happen after a potting is to discover that one of the screens over the drainage hole has shifted in the process of tightening the wire over the root ball. In this dilemma, the bottom soil will start to leak out and form a mound of soil on the turntable below. If not corrected before the soil is watered, air pockets will develop and bottom soil in that area will be lost.

When first observed, this shifted screen can be corrected by crinkling a piece of plastic screen about the size of a marble and forcing it into the hole like a cork. This will keep the soil where it belongs and allow water to drain out of the bottom until the next potting session.

**Delaying tactics.**   If you find your bonsai starting to leaf out at potting time faster than you can get to them, move them to a cool, shady location such as the north side of the house or under cover. Restricting light will tend to extend the dormant period.

## The Elements of Bonsai Styles

Trees in nature are classified genetically by descriptions of the foliage and branching habits such as spreading, conical, pyramidal, weeping, vaseshaped, etc. Bonsai, however, are classified according to the impressions they convey to the observer.

The first of these impressions is size. The very smallest are known as "miniatures" and, oftentimes, occupy pots not much larger than an oversize thimble. The next gradation is the "mame" bonsai which, literally in Japanese, means "palm size," under six inches tall. Others are progressively larger ranging from "small" (six to twelve inches) to "large" (24-inches or more). Then come the oversize specimens, 24-inches or taller. Beyond that are the two-man and four-man giants.

In contrast to the manner with which trees are classified in nature by branching habit and foliage, bonsai are described by "style." As in any creative activity, it is not unusual to identify with a name the form and shape of an artistic result. Then a prototype or pattern is developed for others to follow.

The identification of bonsai "style" as established by generations of Japanese stylists involves the shape and angle of the trunk for single-tree plantings and the number of trees or trunks for multiple-trunk stylings.

There are many different versions of style and each master makes different determinations. John Yoshio Naka identifies some 45 major styles and sub-styles.[1] Style descriptions were simplified by Yuji Yoshimura who classified bonsai into five main styles by their overall shapes, slant of the trunk and orientation of the terminal[2] and this styling version has come into popular use.

Deborah R. Koreshoff details another dozen exotic styles for every conceivable shape and trunk pattern[3] while Dorothy S. Young makes styling distinctions between Japanese and Chinese versions.[4]

Some stylists use the Japanese systems for style classifications and Paul Lesniewicz defines style by their Japanese descriptions, separated by single-tree, multiple-trunk and groups—about fifteen descriptions as found in nature.[5]

Jerald P. Stowell confines his observations to five basic patterns based on Japanese versions,[6] while ten different trunk shapes are analyzed by Kyuzo Murata[7] identified by the Japanese terms. Another Japanese master, Keiji Murata, details twelve styles based on trunk shapes plus root characteristics.[8]

Finally, Wu-Yee-sun, the Hong Kong master of Chinese bonsai, developed two main styling groups: (1) those bonsai that have an ancient appearance and, (2) those with a graceful form.[9]

As in any artform, each expert presents a personal version of style. In some cases, the only differences reside in the language; some descriptions overlap on others; some are exotic and rare and, often, impractical (octopus style, for example).

**The importance of knowing styles.**   For practical purposes, knowing the differences between the various styles enables one to create a particular style with a measure of technical accuracy. While one style sometimes encroaches on another, a recognition that there are styling differences will help to avoid "just-another-tree-in-a-pot" result.

A second reason to learn style characteristics lies in the selection of nursery material for bonsai. It is best to make a preliminary judgment about which style a specimen could best represent before making a purchase. For example, one could hardly plan to style an informal upright version from material that obviously would produce a classical cascade bonsai.

At least learning the vocabulary of the basic forms such as uprights, slanting and cascades will go far to understanding the differences.

**Formal upright.** This is the most difficult style to do correctly because trunk, branching, terminal and roots should follow specific standards. Here are the distinctive characteristics:

- The terminal is aligned directly over the base and curved slightly toward the viewer. There are no bends to the right or left.
- It is a single, upright, straight trunk that tapers gradually toward the top.
- Branches are placed symmetrically around the trunk, usually in groups of three.
- The first branch, either to the left or right, should be heaviest in thickness and the longest in the composition.
- The second branch on the opposite side should be higher, somewhat thinner and shorter in length.
- Branch No. 3 at the back is there to provide depth.
- The lower two-thirds of the trunk should be exposed.
- The top one-third of the composition should taper gently to form a distinct terminal. Usually the top is truncated to keep the height in proportion to trunk thickness, about six times the diameter at the widest dimension. Sometimes the terminal is jinned to finish it off rather than show a stub or inadequate apex formed with a branch (see "The Terminal Problem," page 24).
- All branches should be wired in the same pattern and angulation.
- Strong surface roots must be evident and should be uniformly distributed around the trunk, prominently buttressed.

Formal upright stylings are confined almost invariably to coniferous species, principally pines and junipers, rather than deciduous species such as maples and elms.

**Informal upright.** For individual bonsai, the informal upright style is represented by a curved or slightly slanted trunk and, unlike the formal upright, branching should be asymmetrical. Branches on the side opposite to a curve or slant should be longer. Branches on both sides should be wired parallel to the soil. Lower branches should be wired slightly downward. Like the formal upright, however, the terminal should be positioned directly over the base and slightly curved toward the viewer. A sense of balance must prevail. The design requirements of the informal upright style are not as

rigid as those for the formal upright. This may be the reason why informal upright stylings for bonsai are the most popular. (See Photo Sequence #14).

Twin-trunk and two-tree (father and son, mother and daughter) stylings are handled the same as formal upright except that all branches between adjacent trunks should be removed; branches opposite each other on adjacent trunks should also be avoided.

**Slanting style.** Here, the branching also is asymmetrical as in the informal upright; the angle of slant is more severe but never more than 45° (see Photo #15). The terminal is not positioned over the base, but at a distance from it and it also curves slightly toward the viewer. In other respects, the branching pattern and asymmetrical balance of the informal upright also apply to the slanting style. Branches are wired as parallel as possible to the soil surface, branch tips pointing upward. The more the tree slants, the more the first branch should be lowered as if to counter-balance the composition so it appears to resist the pull from the opposite side.

**Cascade and semi-cascade styles.** To complete the five basic styles where the position of the terminal is the major characteristic, the terminal in the full cascade style goes down below the pot as if the tree grows down the face of an embankment. Here, the pot often is placed on a stand for a full cascaded effect. In the semi-cascade, the terminal curves only to the edge of the pot. As the terminal grows longer, the planting may eventually become a full cascade where the trunk line curves and twists gracefully downward. In both cascade and semi-cascade styles, the tree starts growing upward in the pot with a single branch styled as a formal or informal upright. The trunk then abruptly changes direction and grows downward.

**Asymmetrical balance.** Asymmetry and irregular form are the ways of nature. It is almost impossible for single tree stylings to make bonsai in perfect symmetry, except in the formal upright style. In the latter style, the bonsai is totally symmetrical. If the tree leans or curves to one side, as in the informal upright style, it can be counter-balanced by heavier growth on the other side (see Photo #10). The trunk, therefore, is the most important design compromise. Unless it is thin and pliable, it cannot be changed. Asymmetrical balance and harmony are the disciplines that compensate for shape.

**Group plantings.** These compositions can be styled with formal upright specimens, informal upright, slanting or sinuous configurations—with or without rock outcroppings. Whatever the material, they should resemble a forest wilderness.

Specimens that lack the good qualifications of single

PHOTO #17
Eastern redcedar group, Juniperus virginiana,
41-inches tall, from collected specimens.

*The small trees were collected from an abandoned hayfield where twenty-five years of mowing produced the twisted trunks. The two tallest trees were collected from the hedgerow (see page 72).*

PHOTO #18
Azalea, Rhododendron sp.,
19-inches tall, potted 1974 from nursery stock.

*Root-over-rock style. Over the years, the rock has become an integral part of the root system. The plant has never been separated although it is re-potted and root-pruned every-other-year. The main trunk line shows a straight and uninteresting construction which was concealed with small branches to interrupt the line. It is a vigorous grower. New branches develop in one growing season.*

tree plantings are usually satisfactory candidates for groups. These castoffs may lack buttressed roots, insufficient caliper, awkward branching or uninteresting ramification. When assembled for a group, however, the faults are concealed and they can make impressive bonsai when potted as forests. (see Photo #17).

There are many variations to group plantings ranging from a minimum of three trees to a dozen or more. For styling groups using a relatively large number of trees, an odd number should be assembled, except when ten or more are used, in which case it is acceptable to pot with an even number. When nine or more trees are used in a planting, it is better to style the unit with as few branches as possible to avoid confusion and obscuring trunk shapes. Lower branches can be dispensed with entirely because they will die back anyway for lack of light.

As in twin-trunk styling for single plantings, branches should be removed on the facing surfaces of trunks planted close together. Branches on top that shade other trees also should be removed and, whenever possible, each specimen should have a distinct terminal of varying heights or some terminals should be jinned.

It might seem that such drastic handling of branching in large group stylings would appear bare and uninteresting. On the contrary, groups that involve a relatively large number of trees with varying trunk diameters depend more on the silhouette and movement of the styling rather than branch configuration of individual specimens. Here are other group planting requisites:

• *Use trees of the same species.* While deciduous species sometimes are grouped with conifers, this is not a natural combination in nature. Try to get specimens of the same subspecies and type and which were grown in the same locality. The eye is quick to pick out any inconsistency in a group planting. Select material with different trunk thicknesses and heights to duplicate a natural forest. Adjacent trees should vary in height and thickness throughout.

• *Positioning.* The tallest and thickest tree in the group (the main tree) should be set in an off-center location and it should also be the center of interest, grouped with one or two slender companion trees, shorter and closer together than other trees in the planting. The main tree can also have a jinned terminal. The finished composition should have a triangular outline in silhouette and, unless the sinuous style is used wherein the specimens at the ends point outward, the whole planting should be offset to the right or left.

• *Groupings.* The planting should never be a random arrangement. Trees should be arranged in groups of three. No two trees should be lined up like pegs, but dispersed with unequal distances between them throughout. All the elements must harmonize into a particular theme of movement and produce an impression of a natural scene. Trees should be positioned, selected, or thus wired, with similar curves or positions to suggest that the directions were caused by natural wind conditions. Trees potted on the outside perimeter of the container should be smaller and thinner to suggest that they are younger and they should lean slightly to the outside as if reaching for more light.

• *Stylings.* As in single tree compositions, group plantings can be styled as formal upright groups, informal uprights, slanting or windswept. To create a feeling of perspective, use smaller and thinner trees in the back close to the edge of the container. If the planting is designed as when viewing a forest close up, however, place the smaller trees in front of the larger ones with no tree obscured by another.

• *Wiring.* Wiring for groups is generally a nuisance because ultimate removal is difficult as the material fills out and expands. However, some basic wiring is essential. Group plantings should be arranged in shallow pots to evoke the image of a natural forest scene, often embellished with gravel to represent pathways and rock outcroppings.

• *Ultimate designs.* There is considerable variance in group planting designs, the end result becoming a product of creative skills. Essentially, styling consists of a choice between a tight, single unit with bare soil to the right or left, or several smaller units incorporated into a single composition, or sinuous style where twisted trunks are placed harmoniously to create movement to the right, left or both. (See Photo #17). There is considerable latitude for group plantings as compared with the rigid rules and regulations observed for single specimens. Each master follows a favorite plan. Artistic styling, perhaps, is the best criterion.

**Raft-style bonsai.** The same effect as a "group style" planting can be achieved by removing branches on one side of a formal upright or informal upright specimen and planting it horizontally in a shallow container. Usually, the best branches with interesting shapes are retained. These main branches are positioned upward and, eventually, become individual trees. The original roots should be maneuvered below the soil line or otherwise kept covered so they will function until new roots develop from the new trunks, previously the branches.

Unless the trunk is curved, the new trees developing from the branches will grow in a straight line in contrast to the "group of three" placement as in original group plantings.

**Natural sinuous-style bonsai.** In a land that offers easy access to a rich variety of natural settings, Canadians tend to take the wonders of nature for granted. For example, the most common tree of the Canadian prairie, the black spruce, is a marvel of endurance in the struggle for survival in the wilds.

PHOTO SEQUENCE #19
Hinoki cypress, Chamaecyparis obtussa 'Hinoki,'
potted 1980 from nursery stock.

*While this bonsai suggests a windswept style ("Before"), it cannot be considered a true "windswept" due to the straight trunk emerging from the pot. Also, typical windswept styling requires all twigs and branches windborn in the same direction. The "fanned" foliage of Hinoki is difficult to detail for windswept versions compared with juniper and spruce species where branch terminals can clearly be wired to indicate wind direction. Perhaps this bonsai could better be identified as "windswept-slanting" style. Nevertheless, it illustrates what can be done with material that lacks branching on one side.*

*The lower branch was wired ("After") to visually shorten its length when viewed from the front. The windswept effect probably could also be enhanced by removing the topmost branch and jinning the terminal.*

**BEFORE**                                      **AFTER**

Everything around this unimposing tree seems to conspire toward its extinction. Squirrels clip off its cones; spruce grouse eat the seeds it scatters; matted caribou moss prevents the seeds it does manage to spread from penetrating the soil for germination.

High winds often blow this species from its shallow roots; yet, it will grow on practically bare rock and on the fringes of the tundra. If a black spruce can propagate itself in no other way, its life force is transmitted through its lower branches. When an old tree falls over, the branches send out roots into the soil to become new trees on their own. This is a natural phenomenon of "raft-style" bonsai.

**Rock plantings.** Bonsai can be planted "in" a rock where the rock features openings to hold the soil like a container (see Photo #4) or "on" a rock in the "root clasping" style (See Photo Sequence #18). Never, however, is the rock so dominant that it distracts from the viewer's observation of the tree.

**Windswept style.** "Windswept" is a form of slanting style wherein branches appear only on the windward side of the trunk. Invariably, a bonsai candidate bereft of branches on one side is adapted for a windswept bonsai as a last resort. Actually, some beautiful specimens can be created when nature's forces that suggest the style are analyzed (see Photo #15).

For example, roots should grasp the soil away from the slant as if the tree clings to the ground to support itself—branches and twigs pointing windward should be tightly wired so they are fixed and pointed severely in the same direction as if trained by the wind for generations. Even branches that have appeared to develop leeward should be wired abruptly to change direction windward—and to carry the illusion even further, a branch leeward can be allowed to remain to suggest its time has not yet come.

Ideally, the trunk in the windswept style should be curved in stages to suggest a weakening resistance to the forces of the wind and the bonsai should be potted so it slants in the direction of the wind, although not at too steep an angle—about 30° off center. The terminal should be jinned smoothly and pointed in the wind direction.

Species with characteristically pointed branch ends such as pine and juniper are the best candidates for windswept style rather than species with rounded branch ends such as Hinoki cypress. Deciduous species are never used for windswept style. (See Photo #19).

**Bunjin or "literati" style.** Here is an extreme style which has a character all its own by overstepping established ground rules in trunk taper, branching pattern and treatment of the terminal. While bunjin style generally is selected when no other choices present themselves, there are those who revel in its simplicity with a bare, untapered trunk and a few sparse branches at the very top.

**Broom style bonsai.** The name suggests the appearance of a tree with a branching habit resembling that of a broom—a tree with upward growing branches like elm and zelkova species. The style is characterized by a distinct vaselike or goblet shape and rounded crown as elms grow naturally. There is no back branch. The style is multiple trunked with no dominant terminal. All growth emerges from the same area on the trunk growing upward and outward. It is difficult to find natural material or nursery stock for training into broom style, so admirers of this style usually start material from seed and from well established plants by sacrificing the top portion and starting from scratch. They require many years of careful training. (See Photo #20).

**Styling obsessions.** It is easy to become preoccupied with bonsai styles, especially since one style often encroaches on another. Different teachers observe different standards and refinement details and, sometimes, even individuals who are totally engrossed in bonsai couldn't care less what style is depicted. Sometimes the bonsai candidate itself, while viewed in the ground in the wild or in a can in a nursery, will suggest a style that is natural and appropriate for the species. We must try to hear what the tree is saying. And just as often a slight change in position or rotation will indicate a style that was not immediately apparent.

Regardless of the literal translation of the style in bonsai language, the bonsai always should be a product of its struggle to adapt to an environment. Exposed surface roots suggest soil erosion, driftwood represents wind erosion, jin suggests a disaster, a curved trunk indicates that the terminal successfully sought out a source for sunlight. Indeed, a tree struggling on the side of a cliff for survival becomes a windswept version or cascaded style. Learning the characteristics of styles is an art; delving into the styling details is the discipline.

PHOTO #20
Catlin elm, Ulmus parviflora 'Catlin,'
13-inches tall broom style, in training three years.

*This elm was acquired with an uninteresting, straight trunk 24-inches tall with strong surface roots. The material for conventional styling was unimpressive. The straight trunk, however, made it a likely candidate for a broom style elm.*

*The material was reduced in height to about seven inches. When shoots emerged from the amputated section of the trunk, six weeks after the initial pruning in the spring, about half the shoots were rubbed away. The remaining shoots were allowed to elongate. As pictured, the central shoot was selected to grow rank in order to thicken.*

*There is a tendency, as a result of drastic pruning, for callus to form at the amputated end of the trunk. In order to avoid this, the pruned surface was covered with plastic tape. Signs of callus growth in the spring were filed away. Each autumn, for two seasons, the retained branches were bunched together and tightly wrapped with gauze to establish the typical goblet or vase-like branching habit. In the spring, ancillary branches were shortened and the central branch was allowed to continue with only slight trimming. The photo shows the tree in training for the third season.*

*At least five or six years of continued training in the ground or in a large pot will be required for a conventional broom-style bonsai with ramified branches of variable thicknesses growing upward.*

# 4. *Potting Soils*

Soils in nature store moisture and air in the correct proportions for roots to function. During an environment of dryness, roots penetrate the soil until they reach moisture. If the search for moisture is futile, the plant goes into deep dormancy until moisture is replenished.

In natural surroundings, it may take days or weeks for a plant to react. If moisture becomes available within a reasonable time, the plant recovers from dormancy and dehydration no worse for wear. With bonsai, under the same conditions, the plant may perish. Bonsai in a pot thus must be able to respond quickly to the same demands for moisture and air that the plant encounters in its natural surroundings.

**The soil obsession.** Next to the selection of plant material (See page 51) the physical property of the growing medium is the most important influence to successful bonsai cultivation. Transplanted from the ground, the genetic demands of a plant in a pot are exactly the same as they are in the field, but different problems exist between container grown and field grown plants.

Soil in a container will hold about 20% more moisture than that in the field for these reasons: Containers have limited depth in contrast to the unlimited depth of field soil. Also, a drainage barrier exists in the form of the pot bottom despite the drainage holes. This acts like a layer of rock or shale and creates a "perched" water table—too much water retained below. Many plants cannot survive in nature for long in this environment, nor can bonsai in a pot. Fortunately, there are ways to correct this problem, one of which is to use large soil particles throughout the medium. (See page 52).

**The moist/dry dilemma.** Due to the confined root space in a pot, bonsai soil must still be able to retain some moisture and also have the capacity to get rid of the moisture quickly to replace it with air. If there is such a thing as a perfect medium, it would be described as a soil that retains water for half the time and replaces the water with air for the other half. More specifically, the soil surface should be *moist* to the touch for a period of time following watering and *dry* to the touch some time later. If the soil surface is moist most of the time, something is wrong and should be corrected. Either the

water is not draining away or the soil is not drying out. Determine the limiting factor. Obviously, the timing periods of *moist* and *dry* will vary with sun exposure, wind, humidity and daily temperature. And the soil construction must be adjusted to meet your climatic conditions. Available air in the soil alternated with moisture is the name of the game.

Finally, when water is added to a bonsai pot, the soil should be purged quickly. Water must run freely from the drainage holes. If the water just dribbles away as if it were held back by internal forces, drainage is faulty. And it *is* the internal forces that hold the water back.

**Mechanics of plant growth.** Four major forces enter into the movement of moisture from soil to leaves and back again into the trunk itself. These forces are gravity, adhesion, cohesion and capillarity. "Free water" is that which is held around the roots and not drained away by gravity. Nothing is more detrimental to plant growth than a soil medium that retains too much moisture for too long a period of time.

Thus, as water is pulled away from the soil by the force of gravity, what remains is a thin coating of moisture around each soil particle. This moisture is held by the force of adhesion (moisture molecules clinging to soil, sand and organic particles) and cohesion (moisture molecules clinging to each other). Capillarity is the force that drives the moisture upward where it is used by the leaves to produce nutrients.

Unless there are interspaces in the soil construction, there is no opportunity for free water to be drained away by gravity. When the soil is compacted or the interfaces become clogged with finer material and the forces of *adhesion* and *cohesion* become stronger than the force of gravity, the water does not drain away and the soil becomes sodden.

The more tiny surfaces of soil there are to be coated with water, the worse drainage becomes. Gravity, to move water downward, ceases to function. There are no air spaces left between particles. Free water remains— and this is useless to the roots.

**How roots work.** Roots take up moisture in the form of "vapor," not free water. It isn't the thick, woody roots that perform this function, but the capillary roots, or hair roots, or fibrous roots as they are also called. They are the fine roots at the very tips of thicker roots—root hairs of almost microscopic single cells.

Vapor, which surrounds these root hairs, is a mixture of water and air. Vapor is water in the gaseous state. If the soil becomes sodden with free water and there is no vapor for the capillary roots to absorb—even after gravity has pulled away as much free water as possible—the capillary rootlets cannot respond, or they respond so ineffectually that the plant goes into stress.

Eventually the capillary roots will falter. There will be a gradual decline of foliage which will not be restored until the capillary roots resume their function in the presence of vapor rather than free water.

There are thousands of these capillary rootlets in any pot of soil and, as the capillary rootlets extend, growth above takes place. As each capillary rootlet encounters a soil opening that contains vapor, the rootlet goes on to explore another tiny pocket. The rootlets absorb this vapor by another of nature's forces called osmosis. As the rootlet grows longer, it sends out more capillaries and these, in turn, explore for more vapor and the process continues until a root "mass" is created and the plant flourishes.

These capillary rootlets need the alternating period of moisture in the form of vapor and partial dryness. The extremes are soil that is sodden and soil that is bone dry. This alternate environment of wetness and partial dryness enables the plant to respond with growth. If there is too much wetness, the rootlets will smother; if there is too much dryness, the capillaries will dry out and cease to function. The plant will stress again until new rootlets can be replenished.

In a word, the only water supply available for effective absorption by plant roots is capillary water held around soil particles after gravitational water has drained away.

**Nature's draining mechanism.** The uninitiated may wonder why it is not possible to take ordinary garden soil, transfer it to a bonsai pot, insert the plant and get on your way. The answer is, a good potting medium is not acquired naturally—it is *man-made*.

According to J. W. Boodley of Cornell University, "When field soil is placed in a container, it does not function the same as it did in the field. Nature creates long channels extending from the top soil to the water table below." These are capillary channels that drain out the growing medium and nature, in her wisdom, leaves air space to mix with the moisture that is left. What is more, earthworms constantly tunnel through the soil adding organic matter and creating additional passages for aeration and drainage so water percolates down to the bottom. Nature uses tricks to improve a soil in the ground which we try to duplicate as a growing medium in a pot. So *man-made drainage* must be built into a potting medium to establish vital "vapor."

*Soil Construction*

**The basic mix.** In the early days of bonsai in America, the management of potting soils was a mysterious and complex procedure. Garden loam or topsoil were the principal elements although some authorities advocated the use of clay dug from at least two feet below the soil surface. The loam or topsoil usually were combined with varying proportions of sand and peat moss as amendments to modify water retention capability. The final soil was adjusted depending on the species to be potted, pot size and available sunlight.

This standard mix, which is still used by scores of growers, consisted of one-third each of loam, sand and peat moss. For conifers, an extra portion of sand was added and, for deciduous and evergreen species, an extra portion of peat moss. This was a simple recipe and soils were easy to prepare and store. The synthetic amendments such as Vermiculite, Perlite and Turface were not covered in the few English bonsai texts then available if, indeed, these materials were even in existence. Garden loam, sand and peat moss were the standard ingredients. When such soils became compacted, which happened frequently, the bonsai were repotted and this "fail safe" principal kept plants vigorous.

Today, there probably are as many different potting combinations as there are bonsai growers and all combinations undoubtedly suffice. If the bonsai thrives, produces new growth each season plus fruit and flowers, the potting medium may be considered correct—meaning that the most important characteristic of a "correct" medium is the element of *drainage* for air penetration. Factors such as adequate sun and shade, watering frequency and feeding are contributing cultural requisites, but if drainage is faulty other problems soon follow.

**Particle size is the answer.** Clay (small particles) holds more moisture than sand (large particles). Straight clay soils are not ideal because of poor aeration and slow water penetration; straight sand is not desirable because of poor moisture retention. The amount of moisture retained is governed largely by particle size—and the aim for bonsai is to create a soil mix that holds as much moisture as possible without reducing aeration. The solution is drainage.

**How to establish drainage.** Regardless of the components used, there are two basic requirements for the establishment of good drainage and the creation of "vapor" in the potting medium for bonsai. First, screen out the fine materials that prevent interspaces from being occupied by air and, second, use large enough particles (not smaller than 1/16-inch) so the risk of clogging is reduced.

Soils with large particles (like coarse sand) leave larger open pore spaces and, thus, more air opportunity. Fine-particled soils, having only small spaces (like clay) will be filled with moisture. These soils leave little space for oxygen. Too much organic matter in the form of peat moss or compost will also fill in spaces as they decompose just as much as silt and dust.

Some moisture-retention is required as well as the ability of the soil fully to drain away. This may sound contradictory, but it is possible to construct a soil with such characteristics—highly drainable, moisture-retentive (see "Soil Specifications" page 55). This is accomplished through a balance of large pore openings and small.

Deciduous species and evergreens require more moisture-retentive soils. Conifers which are drought-resistant require soils with less moisture retention. Just as nothing can survive in sodden soils, bone dry soils will never be tolerated by anything that grows except, perhaps, cactus.

**Mechanics of good soil construction.** The use of four screens for sifting is the standard procedure. All components used must be screened—garden soil, peat moss, decomposed granite, volcanic pumice, sand and the synthetic components such as Turface, Terra-Green and Waylite. Selection of these amendments is made according to personal preference and availability.

The screen meshes used are ½-inch, ¼-inch, ⅛-inch and 1/16-inch. An additional screen should be on hand with 1/32-inch openings to eliminate silt and powder from synthetic amendments and sand.* If the 1/16-inch screen is used for this purpose, too much usable material will be wasted. Peat moss and compost, however, can be used after screening through the ¼-inch or ⅛-inch screens.

The ½-inch screen is used to break up soil and peat clods and remove extraneous matter such as pebbles and twigs when garden soil is used as one of the components. It can be omitted for soil substitutes such as Turface which come pre-screened in meshes smaller than ½-inch.

**Acquiring screens.** Screen meshes of ½-inch, ⅛-inch, ¼-inch and 1/16-inch openings can be purchased at hardware stores. They can be cut into convenient squares, mounted with staples on wood frames and assembled as sets. Screen sets about one foot square are easy to handle. For the 1/32-inch screen, it may be possible to procure a small quantity from manufacturers of screen cloth. Or a suitable substitute can be improvised by positioning two 1/16-inch screens so the openings are offset. The new openings then become 1/32-inch.

**How to use the screens.** Stack the screens with the largest openings above. The ½-inch screen is used

*Particle size is identified as material that passes through a specific screen mesh. Thus, material that goes through the 1/16-inch screen and remains on the 1/32-inch screen (after silt and dust are removed) represents 1/16-inch particles.

only for garden soil. Position the stacked screens over a shallow corrugated box or tray to catch the waste. Pour a scoop of soil or soil substitute onto the top screen. The material will pass through the coarse screens quickly after which they can be removed from the stack and set aside.

Shake the remaining screens or push them back and forth until all the material is screened through, repeating the procedure until you have an accummulation of each grade—¼-inch, ⅛-inch and 1/16-inch pellets. The meshes are used separately or combined according to pot sizes and plant species (see "Soil Meshes," page 55). Each lot should receive a final screening through the 1/32-inch mesh screen to eliminate silt and dust. Material that passes through should be discarded.

**Using a screen roller.** For each screen manipulation, lay a piece of one-inch dowel or pipe at the bottom of the box to serve as a roller while moving the screens back and forth. A discarded shower curtain pipe or broom handle is ideal. Cut the roller a little wider than the screen frames.

**Optional screening methods.** It is possible to screen one component so the three principal grades are screened together. To do this, make one pass of soil through the ¼-inch and 1/32-inch screens only. Save what lands on the 1/32-inch screen and discard the rest. This represents a combination of ¼-inch, ⅛-inch and 1/16-inch pellets which is suitable for large pots. For smaller pots, use only the ⅛-inch and 1/32-inch screens.

While sifting soil through four or five screens is good practice, some growers use only the very finest screens (1/16-inch and 1/32-inch) to get rid of silt and dust. This is satisfactory for soil substitutes such as Turface which comes pre-graded, or when the grower starts with small particles for miniature pots.

Some also choose to combine all ingredients into one lot—soil or clay amendments, peat moss or compost, sand and gravel—and then screen the whole collection at one time through 1/16-inch and 1/32-inch meshes. Obviously, there is no control over soil quality with this method since more or less of one or two components in the group may be discarded which will throw all the components out of balance. At the other extreme are those who do not screen soil components at all depending, rather, on a "fail safe" principle of frequent repotting to restore adequate drainage.

Of course, we do not measure these components with scientific precision, but a certain amount of attention to proportions is desirable. And if total screening seems a chore, just remember it is not something you have to do every day. Total screening is little enough insurance that you are at least starting with the correct root environment.

Finally, some theorists have postulated that fine soil encourages root "fineness" and vice versa for coarse soil.

It would appear that these root characteristics, if desirable, are genetic traits rather than a product of soil environment.

## Soil Additives

**Garden soil.** Field soil, loam, garden soil—however identified—are all the same. It consists of decomposed rock, organic matter, silt and clay in varying proportions plus the micro-organisms that convert vegetation and other surface detritus to humus. A large sand content makes the soil friable; a large clay content makes it plastic.

There is nothing wrong with natural soil as a potting medium if it is dug from an area which has not been treated with an herbicide and if air spaces can be created and maintained through the addition of coarse sand. Natural soil, however, eventually will break down and compact due to the high organic matter which eventually decomposes and clogs, in time.

Since all garden soil contains silt and clay the pellets, after screening, are soft and friable. They do not last long in a pot. After a few waterings, the pellets disintegrate and the only material that can keep the soil porous is coarse sand. In the beginning, you will notice the soil holds up well. After a few weeks, the drainage will tend to slow noticeably. The only solution is to repot frequently, change to a larger sand aggregate (fine gravel) or substitute the loam for a fired clay additive (Turface) which will not break down.

Commercial potting mixes purchased in bags at garden centers (Pro-Mix) are intended for house plants. This material is a combination of peat moss and sand. It is too fine for bonsai grown in conventional pot sizes and cannot be screened successfully, although it can be incorporated in the potting mix for small bonsai.

**Synthetic components.** Compared with garden loam, there are many advantages to the synthetic amendments that have come into popular use. They do not compact, they are moisture-retentive and retain good drainage characteristics for long periods of time. The material is uniform lot to lot.

The principle synthetic amendments are Turface, Perlite (kitty litter) and Vermiculite. They are all derived from clay subsoils and fired at high temperatures. Perlite softens in time and loses its structure. It forms unattractive white speckles on the soil surface, floats to the top of the soil during watering and deposits white flakes on pot surfaces. If added to the potting medium, use it sparely—not more than 10% of the mix proportion. Perlite also is very light in weight and lacks the ballast capacity of other clay-like amendments. Ordinary cat litter is similar material, but it has the disadvantage of containing a disinfectant and it should not be used in the potting mix. Terra-Lite, a branded cat litter for horticultural use, contains no disinfectant.

Vermiculite is similar to Perlite that looks like mica. It has tremendous capacity for holding water and its use generally is reserved for seedlings and cuttings.

Turface is the synthetic medium of choice in the experience of this practitioner. It is produced by International Minerals and Chemical Corporation, Mundelein, Ill. It meets all the requirements for a soil amendment for bonsai. Turface is pre-screened and available in two grades, regular and coarse. The "regular" grade represents an aggregate of about ⅛-inch compared with ¼-inch for the "coarse." The regular grade is suitable for all container sizes except the very largest and the smallest sizes.

Turface works directly on the physical properties of soil mixes. Since it is highly absorbent, moisture-retentive properties are maintained while drainage is improved. It acts as a "slow-release" control for moisture. Soils constructed with Turface will seldom dry completely unless watering is thoroughly neglected. If you can visualize a clay flower pot ground up, screened and graded, you will get an idea of the nature of this material. It can be compared with sand in its ballast advantages.

There is another advantage of Turface as an additive. Materials such as loam, peat moss, compost and dried cow manure differ in uniformity throughout the country. Therefore, their particle sizes differ. When conditioning these materials with Turface, the importance of this varying uniformity is minimized.

All the synthetic materials are horticulturally sterile and all should be screened before using by passing them through the 1/32-inch screen to eliminate silt, dust and other fine material that may have accumulated during transportation and handling. This screening can represent a loss amounting to 10% to 15% of the total. Also, since Turface is pre-screened for the standard aggregates, no other screening is required. A material similar to Turface, Terra-Green, also is a clay subsoil mined from a different area.

Since the pH of these fired clay subsoil materials is somewhat above average, potting soils produced with them should be buffered with peat moss for acid-loving plant species such as azalea.

Finally, soil screening to eliminate dust and fines for synthetic materials should always be done outdoors to avoid inhaling the extremely fine particles which can be toxic.

**Humus.** Humus is a natural dark brown substance formed through the decay of plants, roots, insects and the remains of small animals. Decay is caused through the action of bacteria and fungi. The complete humus is compost. Other forms are peat moss, ground bark also identified as "Orchid Seedling Soil," leaf mold and dehydrated cow manure. Many growers avoid the use of these organic substances except when exceptional moisture-retention qualities are required for species such as willow and bald cypress or for acid-loving species as azalea. When these additives decompose, there is a risk that they will fill in the soil interspaces you have tried so hard to create for good drainage.

On the other hand, it is good insurance to add a small amount of organic material (humus, peat moss, ground fir bark, dried cow manure) when fired clay (Turface) amendments are used as the main potting medium. Since synthetic materials lack nutritional elements, a "starter" quantity of some organic matter should be included, about 10% of the mix.

**Sands.** The most important additive to a potting mix is coarse sand which does not hold water. Sand is used to *reduce* water retention. If you use sand that is too fine, you will defeat the purpose of this potting element because it will only clog the other soil interfaces and, rather than improve drainage, it will hamper it.

Sand substitutes can be purchased as parakeet gravel or poultry gravel in various grades. It is important to purchase this material without the calcium ingredient. Poultry gravel or chicken grit, as it also is identified, is available at farm stores. It comes in two grades: starter (fine) and grower grit (medium).

Builders sand can be purchased in bags at garden centers as All-Purpose sand. Screening this material through a $1/32$-inch screen results in waste of approximately 20%. Some growers use this sand as it comes out of the bag. It is inevitable, however, that silt and powder will always remain.

Natural aquarium sand probably is the best source for a coarse material. It can be purchased in pet shops. "Natural" identifies the color. Usually, aquarium sand comes pre-washed and the fine material is floated away. If not pre-washed, it, too, will require screening through $1/32$-inch.

Remember, the identification of sand as "coarse" may not accurately describe the mesh. The term can be applied to many different grades of sand. It is only a relative estimate of size, anyway. If sand fails to pass through the $1/32$-inch screen, it can be considered satisfactory to use. Coarse sand can also be purchased at building supply centers as "traction sand" or "blasting sand." Avoid the material known as "play sand" which is much too fine to use for potting bonsai.

## Soil Specifications

In the early days of bonsai potting, soils were layered by particle size. It was common practice to place a layer of coarse material ($1/2$-inch pellets) at the bottom of the pot on the theory that water accumulation would be reduced through larger interface distances as water percolated downward. It now has been conceded that larger particles on the bottom create a "perched" water condition wherein gravity fails to drain away "free" water.

It makes sense to use the same soil throughout the pot rather than to layer soils in a succession of different textures for bottom soil, main soil and top. The soil mesh should be changed only to accommodate various pot sizes and species requirements. Studies have shown that drainage is defeated when soils of different meshes are used in the same pot. Sometimes roots fail to penetrate through different soil textures creating an "interface" phenomenon that may actually compound the drainage objective.

Soil texture, therefore, is governed, first, by container capacity and, second, by plant species. It stands to reason that the smallest pots for miniature bonsai require the finest soil mesh in the spectrum. Obviously a large pellet, $1/8$-inch for example, in a tiny pot would be useless. And very small pellets in over-size pots would soon defeat the drainage capability. Judgements must be made regarding container dimensions and plant material.

**Soil meshes.** The following specifications apply to pot widths indicated and depths of two-inches.

| For pot sizes (widths) | Pellet sizes (material that passes through the screen meshes indicated) |
|---|---|
| Up to 6-inches | $1/16$-inch screen |
| Up to 8-inches | $1/8$-inch screen |
| 10-inches and wider and cascade pots | $1/4$-inch and $1/8$-inch screens, half-and-half |

**Soil mixes.** The following soil formulas are adjusted for two broad types of bonsai, coniferous and deciduous. For light feeding, drought-resistant conifers, use a small portion of organic matter; for heavy feeding deciduous species and broadleaf varieties (azalea) which require more moisture-retention, use a larger proportion of organic material. Adjustments for greater moisture retention or its opposite, faster drainage, can also be made for geographical considerations, watering habits of the grower and full sun or shade situations. Peat moss improves water retention; coarse sand diminishes it.

| Materials | Species | |
| | Conifers | Deciduous |
|---|---|---|
| Garden Loam or Turface | 1 Part | 2 Parts |
| Builders Sand | 1 Part | 1 Part |
| Aquarium Sand | 1 Part | 1 Part |
| Organic Component (Peat Moss, Humus, Fir Bark) | $1/2$ Part | 2 Parts* |

*Dehydrated cow manure may be used as part of the organic component. If added, reduce the organic component by 50% and replace it with manure.

**Second-hand soil.** Some growers re-use soil for re-potting. There are various disadvantages to this practice: Moist soil violates one of the basic concepts for bonsai potting. Dry soil is friable and fluid and quickly flows around exposed roots, whereas moist soil is bound to leave air pockets. What is more, there is no control over amendment proportions when soil is recovered. Organic matter may have long since decomposed and may have clogged air pores vital to the plant's well being. If used soil is dried completely, however, and then screened through 1/16-inch and 1/32-inch meshes, it may be usable as an emergency medium in training pots or for collected material. It's a small price to pay to take the time and effort to construct new soil for each potting.

**Synthetic mixes and fertilizing.** Since these media are sterile due to the high temperatures with which they are baked, they are weed-free, disease-free and also lack all traces of nutrition when compared with natural soil. This means that they also lack the soil bacteria which decompose organic fertilizers to make the nutrients available to the plant. For this reason, many growers feel it necessary to add a portion of organic material at potting time—at least to have some organic material present in the soil when the roots start to function.

In order to provide a reasonable reservoir of nutrition at potting time, add a portion of garden loam, dehydrated cow manure, commercial potting mix such as Pro-Mix, peat moss, ground pine bark or compost—about 10% of the total. Another option is to add a tablespoon of superphosphate per pot or a palm-down handful of bonemeal for each gallon of soil for an emergency nutrition source until the usual fertilizer regimen is started, usually a month or two after the first potting. Since the additives are from organic sources, they will not "burn" the roots which is the hazard in applying fertilizers too soon when the roots are not yet ready to absorb the elements. While the organic material does provide a modicum of nutrition, it eventually decomposes and this risks clogging air interfaces which the synthetic soil media create.

Newly-potted bonsai in *synthetic* soils can go for some little time on stored nutrients in the plant, but they will require a regular regimen of fertilizing shortly thereafter. Due to the lack of soil bacteria mentioned above that breaks down organic fertilizer formulas, inorganic or "chemical" fertilizers should be used rather than the organics such as fish emulsion, blood meal or bonemeal. In time, however, even synthetic soils acquire windborn soil bacteria and other organisms through the debris which accumulates on soil surfaces.

**Synthetic soil mix advantages.** The first thing you will notice after potting with fired clay materials such as Turface and other derivatives is that drainage is vastly improved compared with a garden loam medium or one using unscreened fine material. Water will run right through and out of the drainage holes. By manipulating particle size for pot proportions and species, perfect drainage can be accomplished and it will last until the bonsai becomes potbound.

Because of the improved drainage characteristics, you may also have to adjust your watering schedule. For example, if your bonsai are kept in full sun (six to eight hours a day of unobstructed sun during the summer months) you may have to water twice a day and fertilize, say, every two weeks with dilute solutions during the growing season.

If available sun is only three or four hours a day or if bonsai are kept in partial shade, once a day watering will be sufficient. Bonsai in small pots, however, should be exposed only to partial sun regardless of the medium to avoid too long a dry period.

So watering and fertilizing habits will have to be changed when you switch to synthetic potting media. But it's a change for the better. You will be pleased when you acquire the knack of constructing soil with super drainage characteristics.

**How to adjust for moisture-retention.** Soil structure can be changed to match your watering conditions and the amount of full sun exposure. For small pots and bonsai kept in full sun, add peat moss or humus to the potting medium. Dried cow manure can also be used, about 10% by volume. For sun exposure of only four or five hours a day, eliminate peat moss. By varying the proportion of ingredients—more coarse sand to increase drainage, more peat moss or compost to increase moisture—it is possible to adjust soil response to your watering convenience and plant requirements.

**Climatic influence on potting soils.** Low humidity and drying breezes will dry bonsai soils faster than high humidity and dead calm. During periods of low humidity it may be necessary to water twice a day; when humidity is high a light spraying of foliage may be sufficient.

**Soil variations.** If water does not drain through the soil quickly and freely by force of gravity, or if it accumulates on the soil surface in small puddles, corrective potting measures should be taken. Likewise, there is no point in constructing a soil with perfect drainage, properly aerated with large particles and easy to assemble if, in the process of potting, overzealous chopsticking breaks down the material to the extent that the resulting silt and powder clogs the interfaces you tried so hard to preserve. It is better to tap the side of the pot with your hand to settle the soil and gently rotate the chopstick to distribute the soil throughout the container rather than using the chopstick as a weapon to eliminate imaginary air pockets.

It would be a simple solution to the potting dilemma if we were able to construct a single mix for all bonsai, young and old and for all species from deciduous to coniferous, all climates and all pH requirements. This, however, is not practicable. Old bonsai do not respond the same as young; older bonsai are more flexible in their requirements for nutrients and water because they have developed larger and more efficient storage and distribution systems; and different species have different genetic moisture requirements.

Each situation requires a measure of analysis and each bonsai you pot may be just a little different in some respects than the one you did before or the one coming next. Soil compositions and proportions must be adjusted to match the requirements. This is creative potting.

Bonsai potting soils should not be considered a mysterious and complex subject that requires a liberal education to master, nor is it difficult to create the perfect potting medium when the simple objectives are kept in mind together with the reasons thereof. A plant needs moisture in the form of water vapor plus nutrition and sunlight; roots need air and water to execute their functions. These are the elements nature provides in abundance in a natural environment.

**Soil deception.** When you repot, don't be afraid to use an ample measure of sand or other sharp aggregate in your mix. Dry soil containing a large amount of organic matter may appear granular, but the organic material will break down by the end of the growing season and compact. Extra sand will compensate for this.

**Strange soil environment.** All soils started from rock, volcanic dust, pumice and other detritus. The hard material such as rock was worn down by glaciers, pulverized and transported by water and wind, to be laced with organic material resulting in soil.

Sometimes a particular type of soil supports one plant and no other. At an elevation of 9,000 feet in the White Mountains of Eastern California grow the ancient bristlecone pines, perhaps the oldest living things in the world. These forlorn trees grow profusely in coarse, broken dolomite rock with little or no visible soil in the area. The desolate environment and impoverished soil supports very few grasses or other vegetation. And yet, the bristlecone refuses to grow in fertile areas where soil and humus have accumulated or in areas not covered with the dolomite rock.

Bonsai is not the only thing growing that is fussy about soil environment.

**Screening rules and regulations.** No matter what soil composition you use, all materials should be screened to eliminate powder and fine particles. A perfect soil atmosphere could be considered as 50% solids, 25% air and 25% moisture. This ideal proportion applies for bonsai already growing in a container. Since we pot with bone-dry material, the 25% moisture allocation is taken up with air, making the ideal dry mixture 50% solids and 50% air. Particles under $1/16$-inch will reduce this air proportion by fitting themselves into the interspaces. That is why all screened materials, even peat moss, passing through $1/16$-inch screen should be discarded. Material that passes through the $1/16$-inch screen and accumulates on the $1/32$-inch screen should be used for the smallest pots only. Peat moss and compost can be considered satisfactorily screened by using material that passes through the $1/4$-inch or $1/8$-inch screens.

**The interface problem.** Changing soils without considering the mysterious characteristics of roots that fail to penetrate a new medium can result in retarded root growth. When a potting medium is changed, say, from a loam mix to a medium containing processed clay additives, the roots must quickly adapt to removing moisture from a strange, surrounding soil. To encourage the transition, expose the roots out of the old rootball about an inch to break through the interfaces of different soils and textures. Expose the root ends so they will be in contact with the new medium.

**Different soils, same pot.** If you change the soil composition at repotting time, it should be done gradually by removing pie-shaped wedges from the rootball over a period of several growing seasons. This is especially important for established bonsai that have been growing successfully in the same soil mix for several years.

Changing soil abruptly not only alters the environment around the roots, but the portion of old soil clinging through the rootball may have a different moisture-retention quality than the new material. Result: If you water for the old soil, part of the new medium may be too dry; if you water for the new soil, the old soil may stay too moist. Wedging new soil into the old ball equalizes the changeover gradually.

Meanwhile, when you water, touch the ball containing the old soil and compare the dryness of the new soil. Water only that portion which is dry until roots enter the new medium and moisture requirements for the new soil catches up.

**Clogged drain holes.** If all potting components are screened and the particle sizes are large, perfect drainage should be accomplished from the very beginning. Occasionally, and as the season progresses, the drainage may falter. Sometimes compacted soil is not the reason for faulty drainage. Inspect the drainage holes. They can easily become clogged and impair drainage. Simply poke a few larger holes in the screens and use a coarser screen to cover the holes when next you repot.

**Restoring settled surface soil.**   The soil surface in containers should be about ¼-inch below the container lip in order to allow for accumulation of water to seep into the root ball. Sometimes the soil settles and this space becomes more than enough to serve as a funnel for the water. Also, this extra space makes the soil surface appear untidy and unfinished.

Rather than add more soil to the top which would cover the surface roots and moss, cut the wire which secures the root ball on the bottom of the pot, lift the ball out of the pot and add the extra soil to the bottom to raise the level to the desired height. Use the same bottom soil mix as the original potting. Once the roots have become established, the plant need no longer be secured in the pot with wire.

**Loam vs. synthetic media.**   One of the advantages of fired clay soil amendments compared with screened garden loam is the greater stability of the synthetics. Loam pellets disintegrate quickly if you are not careful to avoid compacting the soil during potting. They also tend to break apart as a result of watering. Fired clay particles are more lasting.

**Avoiding deadly mistakes.**   Make one or two common errors in potting, pruning, care and feeding and you might get by with no serious consequences. But if you compound the mistake, you may get into trouble. For example, you might get away with it if you use too little sand in potting drought-resistant pines and junipers. That's mistake Number One. If you are careful how often you water, the mistake can be neutralized. But if you compound the error by overwatering, watch out.

**Soil sterilization.**   There's no need to heat small quantities of soil in the oven to get rid of soil-born insects and fungi. Simply place the soil in a tightly sealed black plastic bag and set it in full sun. Puncture a few holes in the bag or the expansion of moisture may rupture the bag. Turn the bag every few hours to heat the contents uniformly. The inside temperature gets as high as 180° to 200°F. which is about what you need for oven sterilizing. Four or five days in the full sun and you have sterile soil.

**Drainage dilemma.**   When bonsai are first potted and you are careful not to compress the soil with too much jabbing, the drainage appears to be just about perfect. As the season progresses, you may find that the drainage gets sluggish. Try to determine the reason: (1) too much fine material that has clogged interspaces, (2) hardened organic material on the soil surface as a result of fertilizing, (3) compaction through heavy rain or watering. If the soil composition is too fine, this can be altered at the next potting through coarser materials; if the faulty drainage is caused by compaction at the soil surface, cultivating lightly with a chopstick will correct the situation.

Drainage can also be impaired through the application of too much moss. The soil surface should never be completely covered. This looks unnatural, conspicuous and can also impede the entry of air.

**Compaction study.**   According to Prof. J. W. Booley of Cornell University, a study in Florida showed that compaction of a peat-Perlite medium in small plastic pots greatly affected root and shoot growth of two foliage plant types. Root growth in the non-compacted medium was four times greater than plants growing in compacted soils. Shoot growth was 50% greater on plants growing in non-compacted soils.

**Crusty soil.**   Along about the middle of summer, you may notice that the surface of the soil in pots uncovered by moss often becomes hard, brittle and compacted. This is apparent when the soil surface is dry. While water may penetrate freely, this crusty surface impedes air circulation. Loosen the soil surface gently with a chopstick so it becomes friable. Score the soil around the pot edges, too. You'll notice quite a difference in drainage with this simple procedure.

**When to use fine soil.**   The fine soil or silt that passes through the ¹⁄₃₂-inch screen ordinarily should be discarded. It is not suitable for use in a potting medium because it ultimately will work its way between coarse particles and produce a compacted environment. Before discarding the fines, save a cupful or two to sift around moss and lichen on the soil surface. A very small quantity should be used—just enough to fill in the gaps between moss and lichen patches.

**Correcting poor drainage.**   If poor drainage is evident and it is impossible to repot, a temporary correction can be made by poking holes carefully in the soil with a chopstick. The holes may fill up again within a short time, however, and the procedure may have to be repeated until potting time comes around again and a soil mix with better drainage capability can be used.

Another solution to poor drainage is to water less frequently. Ordinarily, bonsai should be watered only when the soil surface is dry. Of course, there is no way of knowing how wet it is below, but if you allow the soil to stay dry an extra day before you water, the roots will help deplete the excess moisture through transpiration. Another suggestion is to keep the bonsai in full sun so it dries out faster.

Removing soil from the edges and corners of the container without disturbing the roots and replacing the soil with sand will also help correct poor drainage to some extent.

**Drainage and watering.** Poor drainage and overwatering are common faults and they are closely related. If drainage is good, you can actually over-water (both by frequency and volume) without serious consequences. If drainage is inadequate, you can suffer a situation where the soil is too wet too long even with a reduced watering schedule. Preparation of a potting soil for bonsai to flourish is a skill in itself.

**Planning ahead.** If you store garden loam for future use and screening, dig it out while the ground is friable and before leaves fall and obscure the surface. Store the freshly dug soil in trays or pails where they won't get rained on. By the time you are ready to screen it, the loam will be nice and dry and ready to process.

# 5. Trimming–Pruning–Pinching

As Shakespeare observed, "Man is the paragon of animals," so bonsai has been described as the "highest form of horticulture." You can easily succeed in areas of horticulture other than bonsai by providing the four major basics: light, water, air and fertilizer. If a plant growing outdoors or a houseplant on a windowsill starts to falter, it probably will regain its vigor if you can determine the cause of stress. If the plant is exposed to less sunlight than the species genetically requires, moving the specimen to another area may restore it; if irrigation is deficient, you simply turn on the sprinkler or water more often to rectify the situation; if the plant looks languid, fertilizer may revitalize its color and well being. Given time and attention, it is relatively easy to succeed with yard or houseplants. Not so with bonsai.

### Care and feeding vs. training and styling.
Bonsai exist in an artificial microcosm. They are indulged and showered with care. They are supposed to have every horticultural characteristic of vigor and, yet, appear as if they endured a hardship. In addition to the factors that contribute to a clean bill of health and robust appearance—and in contrast to yard and houseplants—bonsai involve much more than administering to the plant's basic needs. Time and attention must be devoted to training and styling—and this never ends.

All the functions of training and styling involve roots, trunk, branches and foliage—the variety and size of the branches in relation to the trunk—even the placement of the tree in the pot. If these training functions are missing and you are satisfied without the perfection of bonsai design, then there is no problem. Any woody material growing in a pot will do. It is not neglect that creates a naturally-weathered and venerable appearance, but the bonsai *technique*—knowing what to train, bend and trim, what to leave alone and what to convert to jin and driftwood. *Trimming*, *pruning*, *pinching* are the functions that determine the future shape and beauty of the specimen.

### Branch ramification.
Old trees growing in nature are distinguished by a network of branchlets and twiggery. It is an aging characteristic analogous to "wrinkles" in aged people. There is a difference in the trimming, pruning, pinching techniques, although they all lead to the same goal: To encourage the multiplication of an offshoot to produce more branches—which produce more twigs—which foster more twiglets—and so on to many orders of growth. Eventually, a sparse, immature-looking bonsai will develop a top appearance that resembles a tree of considerable age. Trimming, pruning, pinching is a patient, long-term process. There is no single, drastic operation that will accomplish the same purpose. And the reward is a growing thing of artistic quality.

### Mechanics of plant growth.
Buds on branch tips and surfaces which develop during the growing season represent next year's potential growth. These buds are very apparent. In coniferous species, they consist of light green growth on the very tips of branches and branchlets. They are "candles" in pines, "tufts" in spruces and taxus, "fans" in Hinoki cypress and "scales" or "needles" in junipers. New growth also arises in axils and internodes of some conifers and most deciduous species, especially maple and elm.

A single bud on a branch contains all the genetic chromosomes of the species. A bud often will grow in the direction it points which is a handy characteristic for bonsai styling. If not removed, a bud eventually will elongate into a branch—an important fact to remember when dealing with maples, elms or other fast growing species, especially when you need a replacement branch or one to fill in a design fault. (See Photo Sequence #21).

### New branch.
It is possible to force a bud to develop into a branch more quickly rather than waiting for it to develop naturally. Make a horizontal cut in the trunk *below* the bud you want to develop. This cut interferes with the flow of nutrients up from the cambium layer and down through the phloem tissue and forces the nutrition to the nearest point above the cut—which is the dormant bud you want to develop. When the cut heals, the bud will continue to grow.

Then there are the adventitious buds which are barely apparent on the branch surfaces. They hide under the bark waiting for a fortuitous opportunity to emerge. If branch tips are destroyed by frost or browsing animals,

## PHOTO SEQUENCE #21
Japanese redleaf maple, Acer palmatum rubrum,
21-inches tall, potted 1982 from nursery stock.

*While this bonsai features desirable surface roots and buttressing, the trunk lacks curves or other interesting characteristics. In addition, the terminal shows a bad surrogate extension which detracts from the design potential ("Before").*

*During wiring, the main branch on the left cracked. The ends were wired together in an effort to create a graft, a procedure often successful with fast-growing maples. The graft never matured, however.*

*In desperation, the remaining stump was pruned close to the trunk. The following growing season, several buds appeared at the point of amputation. One bud, pointing in the correct position, was selected to elongate without pinching or pruning. The branch eventually extended to about two feet with corresponding thickness. The new branch finally was pruned back to proportion ("After")—a complete, new branch where the original branch once grew. The branch was wired and trimmed and a branch in the upper terminal was trained to conceal the awkward juncture.*

**BEFORE**                    **AFTER**

these dormant buds go into action. They are nature's emergency measure for survival and they are activated when a hormone, auxin, in the branch tips is removed by accident or design. In effect, this hormone in the branch tip monitors new growth below. When the tip is removed, the adventitious buds are signaled to grow.

For all species, ramification or branching fretwork is accomplished through constant attention to *trimming, pruning, pinching.* These functions should always be done from the front of the bonsai. In addition to wiring, they are the tools of styling. Here are the basics of the three grooming procedures:

**Trimming** is the process of reducing elongated growth. Branches that have grown beyond the design profile should be trimmed back. Inside branches and new growth that develop at internodes and axils should also be removed. When these areas are reduced through trimming, more light and air reaches the crown. The shape of the bonsai is not altered when trimming is moderate and attended to periodically. Light and air inside branch structure are a rejuvenating process that channels the plant's energy into the remaining branches to enhance ramification. When pruning is neglected, however, and branches outgrow the design, you court a styling disaster (see Photo Sequence #22).

Branch die-back due to lack of sunlight is nature's way to eliminate branches that perform no function for the wellbeing of the tree, but they may be ever-so-important to the bonsai design and style. Trimming should be done with a small scissors because it often involves cutting into thin, woody portions.

Wherever possible, a branch should be trimmed so a free growing bud remains at the tip, preferably in the direction you wish to encourage growth. This is easy to observe in species such as pine, spruce and taxus, but juniper and cypress species are not as apparent. In deciduous species, trim just above the active bud, leaving a small amount of old wood to avoid injury to the bud you want to develop.

**Pruning** is a more drastic maneuver than trimming that not only alters the shape of the tree, but also helps to channel a plant's energy to where you want it either for horticultural or esthetic reasons, or both. Branches that have died back, however, frequently are retained and jinned to be used as part of the styling scheme if they are in a suitable location.

Thinning interior branches increases light and air penetration to the crown which improves vigor (see Photo Sequence #14).

The best time for drastic pruning is in early spring before new growth starts. When removing entire branches, cuts should be made directly in front of the branch collar, the ridged area that encircles a branch close to the trunk. This may leave a spur that may offend some esthetic standards, but the callus growth

will be faster and, in time, the knot will become part of the trunk structure. Don't bother to treat the wound with a tree-wound paint. Trees have been responding effectively to their wounds for over 200 million years. If the newly pruned wood is too prominent, smear a little soil over it to conceal it or apply Chinese ink with a paint brush.

If drastic pruning is carried to excess or performed incorrectly, the amputations can devitalize a bonsai, create stress and set it back in development for several growing seasons until it has had a chance to recuperate.

**Pinching** is a refining process that involves removal of the growing tips also identified as "candles," "tufts," etc. This is best accomplished with the thumbnail or a twisting action of the thumb and forefinger. If it is difficult to reach pine candles with fingers and thumbnail, use tweezers to twist the candle off. Breaking off the candle is better than crushing the needles with a scissors. Remove from one-third to one-half of the candle. In this way, a few needles will remain at the candled base for future development.

If needles have developed out of the candle and are starting to spread open, it is too late to pinch back and the only option is to remove the entire stem.

Tufts of spruces are removed by separating the outer needles with the thumbnail and removing the inner portion. If the outer needles are pinched they will turn brown. In taxus species, the entire tuft can be removed. In spruces and taxus species, if the needles have opened, the branch will elongate.

In chamaecyparis and juniper species, new growth is continuous and can be pinched back at any time during the growing season. Simply grasp the branch ends between thumb and forefinger of one hand as a barber would do in trimming hair and, with the other hand, using thumb and forefinger, pinch off the light-colored new growth.

For deciduous species, unwanted buds can be rubbed off. Terminal buds that have grown into branchlets can be reduced to one or two nodes with scissors. Varieties of maple that are well established can be controlled by picking out the fresh, new growth between the older leaf sets.

**Deciduous species pruning summary.** Deciduous species are faster growers than pine, juniper and other conifers and are remarkably responsive to a summer regimen of training. Once the details of procedure are learned through practice, the results of ramification are rewarding.

If buds on a branch are spaced too widely, nip out all the buds except the one nearest to the trunk. If a branch has buds at close intervals, nip only the buds that grow in unwanted directions. By focusing on one bud that will enhance the design either on a branch or branchlet, its growth will be accelerated by removing the com-

PHOTO SEQUENCE #22
Prostrate juniper, Juniperus squamata 'Prostrata,'
18-inches tall, potted 1976 from nursery stock.

*A portion of the trunk of this specimen was destroyed by borers. In the spring of 1983, the infestation caused the plant to decline and it almost perished. The wood was treated with chlordane, gouged out and bleached for shari. All styling and pinching were suspended and the branches were allowed to grow wild ("Before"). The bonsai became thick and overgrown. Two seasons were lost in the training schedule.*

*In the spring of 1985, the branches were drastically pruned and thinned. When junipers grow rank through neglect or for re-styling and subsequently are drastically pruned, a profusion of juvenile growth develops. This specimen was no exception. There was little choice in the strategy for improvement.*

*The branches were re-wired and shaped ("After"). The open branching revealed the trunk shape from base to terminal. It was trimmed and fertilized lightly to discourage additional juvenile growth. With the shape restructured to allow light to enter inside, new whipcord needles started to replace the juvenile growth. The restyled photo shows the bonsai in the spring of 1986.*

**BEFORE**

**AFTER**

petition. If a branch has grown rank because bud-nipping was neglected, prune off the undesirable portion and start over again. Trim deciduous species often during the growing season. Use scissors or, when young, use fingers.

For additional details on trimming, pruning and pinching see *Species Specifics*, page 67.

**Growth rates vary.** Buds should be pinched according to their rate of growth. Not all evergreens are pruned at the same time nor in the same manner. Pines, firs and spruces produce only one surge of growth during the year. Most other evergreens such as juniper, yew and hemlock continue to develop during the growing season. If left untouched, the branches will grow rank, the plant will grow out of proportion and the interval between twigs will be too long (see Photo Sequence #22). In contrast, when a branch is virtually "nipped in the bud" by reducing the terminal end, the result is the development of lateral twigs. When lateral twigs are pinched again, they form more laterals and branchlets. Finally, a network or complexity of growth is established which is highly prized in bonsai. This is *ramification*.

When the three major basics—light, water, fertilizer—that encourage good, new growth are present, you will get at least one opportunity to pinch and trim each growing season. In southern California where the growing season is about ten months of the year compared with three or four months in the Eastern states, they get two and sometimes three orders of growth each year. That is why bonsai in California look so much further advanced. And when we compare bonsai in this country with their counter-parts in Japan, the most striking contrast resides in branch ramification and the results of patient and thoughtful nipping for years and, often, for generations.

**Pinch all sides.** There is a tendency during the pinching and trimming procedures to concentrate exclusively on the front of the bonsai and those branches which are the most prominent and easiest to handle and to get at. Don't neglect the back branches on the premise that they do not contribute to the overall styling. Back branches lend depth to a planting. They should be groomed and styled just as much as the more prominent elements in the design.

**Grow and clip styling.** While immediate shaping results are apparent through wiring, some individuals either lack the wiring skill or find the presence of wire distracting. To insure a fixed position of a branch, wire must often be left on for as long as a year and some species are even resistant to wiring. Spruces have this unfortunate characteristic. In these cases, the "Grow and Clip" technique (Lingnan method) developed by the

Chinese is a perfect solution if one has the patience to wait for the final result.

The "Grow and Clip" procedure involves shaping by pruning exclusively, without the use of wire. Here is how it works: A branch is allowed to develop, sometimes for years. When it is nipped, adventitious buds will sprout in different directions and a new side branch will develop. The new branch is retained and the original branch is severed at that juncture. When the side branch has again developed for a year or more to the desired thickness, it, too, is nipped to encourage a second side branch to grow and so on. The procedure is repeated until a picturesque configuration is attained. Branch movement can also be altered with the Lingnan technique. For example, a branch growing upward can be made to grow downward by cultivating a stem in that direction—all with no wire. It is a purist and long-time procedure, but exquisite bonsai can result. Branches can also be trained without wiring by tying them down to pots with string or thin wire, or through weights.

**Small leaves.** Bonsai beginners worry about how to achieve small foliage for esthetic proportions. Foliage does not "shrink up" shortly after a plant is placed in a pot. Small foliage is a refining result—a dwarfing mechanism which takes hold years after bonsai are well established. Smaller foliage materializes with *adequate*, not *over*-fertilizing—*adequate*, but not *over*-watering—close attention to the pinching and pruning process and, finally, the length of time a plant is in a pot. Paradoxically, leaves reduce in size with proper care and culture, but fruit and flowers always stay the same size as in a natural environment.

**Concealing a new pruning scar.** A branch severed from the trunk often leaves a prominent light-colored scar until it heals and calcifies. The usual procedure is to carve out the area to make it concave and allow the calcification process to fill it in.

Until the scar darkens with age, it can be concealed with Chinese ink which can be purchased in stick form at any art supply shop. To use, glide the stick around a small clay saucer to which a few drops of water have been added. The ink is dark gray and blends with most bark colors. Apply with a brush. The color can be varied from light to dark by grinding in more ink.

**Shaping branches.** When trees are in full foliage, it is difficult to apply wire without damaging the leaves. If the shaping requirement is merely to lower the branch, it is better to tie the branch down with thin wire fixed to another wire around the container.

**Juniper branch training.** Without wire, the branch tips of junipers grow naturally upward toward the sun. If you wire a branch pointing *downward*, the tip will be locked in this position and, unable to reach for the sun, the branch will die back to the point where the tip can point upward again. Always, therefore, point the tip toward the sun when you wire. If lower branches are shaded by upper branches, the latter should be wired out of the way so the lower branches will receive sunlight.

**Creating a new branch.**    Maples and azaleas sprout readily from old wood on trunks and branches. Should a branch be badly angled or in the wrong place, pinch it back frequently to encourage budding nearby. Then select the bud that appears to be the most suitable. It won't be long before it becomes a surrogate branch to the one rejected. Conifer species sprout from old wood occasionally, but they are not as reliable as deciduous species. Hinoki cypress never sprouts from old wood.

**Styling never ends.**    Pinching, trimming, thinning out is a continuous process, but the rewards are manifold. "Finished" bonsai allowed to become thick and overgrown usually develop die-back on inside branches. Without light, there will be empty spaces. Thinning the outside allows light to enter inner foliage.

**Winter shaping.**    The best time to wire and shape deciduous material is when the bonsai have defoliated. Not only is branch structure clearly visible, but it is also easier to wire during dormancy when buds are small and tight. When buds swell in the spring, they can be easily wiped off. Any winter work should be done outdoors. Bringing them inside out of dormancy, even for an hour, may encourage the plant to break dormancy which may result in winter-kill of the new, tender growth. After winter wiring and shaping, keep them out and protected until all danger of frost has passed.

**Quick callus formation.**    Callus growth in large wounds which have already callused over somewhat can be hastened by trimming the edge around the ring of callus tissue from time to time. Repeated injury stimulates additional growth to fill in a pruned area.

**When to leave the branch alone.**    To thicken a branch, do not trim. The longer the branch is allowed to grow, the thicker it will become. The bonsai may grow lopsided for the growing season, but the results are worth it. Also, avoid late summer pruning (August through September). Pruning at this time of the year encourages new growth to develop which may not harden off sufficiently for winter thereby increasing the danger of winter injury.

**On thickening trunks.**    For a bonsai with inadequate taper, this deficiency sometimes can be corrected by cultivating the material in the ground and in full sun for two or more growing seasons. The effect can be stimulated by planting it deeper than usual. Partially

"strangling" the trunk just below soil surface will cause the trunk to swell and that also helps correct the stick-like look. Another trick is to let suckers or low growing branches grow unrestrained during the two-season in-ground period. The trunk will thicken below this growth.

**Grafting trunks together.**    If you have three saplings, none of which will make suitable bonsai because of thin stems and sparse foliage, try grafting them together. Scrape off a strip of bark on one side of each of these mavericks about two-thirds of the lengths starting at the roots. Bind all three trees together with the bare sections pressing tightly against each other. If the trunks are flexible, they can be bound with florists' tape or nylon strips. The tighter you bind, the better the results. Do not use wire. The saplings will grow together in time into a creditable single-trunk specimen.

**Thickening terminals.**    To thicken a surrogate terminal formed by wiring a branch upward, allow new shoots on this branch to grow wild. The new terminal will thicken quickly. Cut the branches back in the spring and allow them to lengthen again to repeat the process.

**Creating foliage close to trunks.**    For coniferous species that lack branches close to the trunk, snip off the branch end and side graft it to the same branch where you need more foliage. Wedge the scion with a razor blade, insert it into a cut in the branch and bind with grafting tape or plastic tape. A grafted branch should never be wired. Remove the tape after vigorous growth is observed.

**Styling disaster.**    Great care is devoted to styling a newly potted bonsai. Every twig and branch is wired in place to fulfil our vision of perfection. Then what happens? We either forget or neglect to pinch or prune during the growing season to retain the shape we tried so hard to create.

Should this occur, start over again next season. (See Photo Sequence #22.) It's best to maintain only a few bonsai and give each one a full measure of attention rather than nurture a collection of overgrown potentials.

**Growing tip dilemma.**    During the fast growing season, almost all new shoots grow either straight up or straight into the center of the tree. The tips reach for light and they will grow inside the plant as long as light is not obscured. There is a strong tendency to clip off anything growing in the wrong direction just to get rid of it. This wastes branchlets that would add to ramification. After the tips elongate, wire them into the proper configuration. This takes time and effort, but the result in a more finished-looking bonsai is worth it.

**Putting them out to graze.**    The trunks of bonsai

in pots are always thinner than those of trees of similar age growing in the ground because nature preserves a balance between the root system and the parts we can see. Bonsai given a respite in the ground to increase trunk girth will also develop a root system unmanageable for a pot. It is possible to restrict the depth in the ground to which roots will penetrate and, at the same time, increase trunk thickness and side growth. When putting them out to "age," dig a wide and shallow hole. Place a tile, flat rock or a piece of plastic at the bottom of the shallow hole and cover it thinly with soil. Position the roots so they radiate outward and fill the hole with soil. When you are ready to replace the tree in a pot, you will have a manageable root ball requiring only moderate trimming of the side roots.

**Timing the pruning procedure.**    Pinch and trim when new growth is apparent, and when branches have grown to one or two nodes. Otherwise, you may also remove a microscopic reservoir of hormone at the branch tip that monitors growth below it and which may not yet have received the signal. This hormone in the tip of a branch that has started to grow controls the budding below it. As long as the tip is undisturbed, the branch will elongate. When the tip containing the hormone is removed, the adventitious buds go into action. There is no 100% guarantee that every cut and pinch will result in more vigorous branching, but waiting until the branch has elongated before pinching and trimming will increase the odds.

**Growth habits.**    Maples will bud out close to existing branches. If you have a branch not quite in the ideal position, cut it back until new buds appear on the trunk nearby. Then select one bud that is in the desired spot, wait until it becomes well-established and then prune away the old branch.

**The penalty of neglect.**    At the end of summer, it is easy to observe which bonsai have been neglected from the standpoint of pinching and trimming. Deciduous species are the most obvious with long internodes, crossing branches and branches growing inward. Coniferous species lose old needles in back of new growth. Junipers become scraggly and unkempt when pinching is neglected and pines develop a long, thin branch with an unattractive tuft at the end of it. When the pinching process is neglected for a season, the only other option is to cut the branches way back which results in unnatural-looking stubs at the branch ends. Unfortunately, a whole season of ramification has been lost. Inspect your bonsai before you put them away for the winter. If you see evidence of added twiggery, you have done your homework; if the internodes are long and if the branching habit is sparse, pay closer attention to the pinching and trimming process when you have the best opportunity to do it—during the growing season.

**Maintenance trimming.**    "Maintenance" procedures apply mostly for mature bonsai. Trimming branches to one or two nodules during the growing season usually suffices for finished bonsai in order to retain styling, but this will never do for undeveloped branches on newer bonsai, say, under two or three years in a container. For these specimens, it is better to allow undeveloped branches to grow freely and fatten up even if the bonsai appears awkward for a while. It takes time for bonsai to acquire a finished look.

**Leaf pruning.**    This is a common practice used to increase foliage and reduce leaf size in deciduous species, especially elm and maple, except dissectum cultivars, and species grown for flowers, fruit and berries. The bonsai to be leaf-pruned should be well-fertilized two weeks before trimming to make certain there will be adequate nutrition to restore foliage. Remove the leaves during June and July by clipping the stems. Be careful to avoid injury to stem buds which are situated close to the branch, otherwise a new leaf will not grow in that spot. For conservative leaf-pruning procedures there are three options: (1) defoliate only the largest leaves, (2) remove only half the leaves on a stem or, (3) cut each leaf in half. In the last option, the leaf left on the branch will fall off when the new leaf emerges. The result of leaf pruning will be vigorous growth, better secondary branching and improved color. Water sparingly until new leaves grow back and do not fertilize again until new leaves are well established. Vigorous growers can be leaf-pruned two or three times during the growing season.

**Avoid hasty pruning.**    Allow a first flush of new growth to develop after potting to stimulate root activity. Unwanted growth can be pruned away later and second growth response will be more vigorous. Resist the urge to style the bonsai in its final form immediately upon potting. While the general configuration can be established, the new growth will better suggest the future styling.

At the other extreme, many bonsai beginners fail to trim top foliage hard enough. This results in tops that are too bushy and lower branches that are weak and sparse. Maples, especially, require drastic heading back of top growth.

# 6. *Species Specifics*

**Climate orientation.** Some bonsai growers become disappointed when they try to cultivate plant species from distant temperature zones, even with adequate measures to insulate the plant against extreme cold (see "Winter Protection").

Hardiness zones, as defined by the U.S. Department of Agriculture, are determined by "average minimum temperatures." The lower the zone number, the lower the coldness factor. Species that flourish in zone seven, for example, and maintained in zone six will have to contend with much more than the freezing risk. The answer is "*microclimate.*" It is the sum of all the natural conditions and influences that affect the life and development of a plant to be conditioned for bonsai.

Microclimate includes intensity of sun exposure, rainfall, humidity and dryness. In the mountainous, desert area of California where the California juniper thrives, there is bound to be some difference in the species' response and vigor when it is transferred to another zone, say, the East. In its natural environment the species does receive some freezing exposure for a short period of time during the year, but the microclimate also is characterized by a broiling sun, long dry spells, low or no humidity and low annual precipitation.

In contrast to the air dryness in its natural area, the juniper in the East must endure prolonged periods of humidity and moisture during the summer when, in its natural environment, it goes into dormancy. The opposite microclimate conditions prevail with species such as buttonwood, native to Florida, and bald cypress conditioned to the climate of Louisiana. Texas elm, which prospers in a totally different set of survival requirements, does not perform well when transplanted away from its genetic environment (see Photo #23).

Nevertheless, many growers do maintain such species, although not ideally, in seemingly hostile surroundings. The plants demand special attention to soil composition, watering frequency and sun exposure. The limiting and most serious factor is the humidity. Even with prudent precautions, species transplanted from one zone to another do not thrive in vigor and appearance compared with the way they look in their natural microclimate environments.

**Pines.** This is the easiest species to reduce and keep in trim because the material to be pinched away is readily apparent. New growth at the ends of pine branches elongates and resembles candles, so removal of this new growth is called "candling." Head back the candles in the spring as they emerge and before they unfold into obvious needles. This will establish dense growth.

The easiest procedure is to cut each candle in half with a small scissors, leaving a cluster of needles to continue to grow and produce new foliage. Instead of a small scissors, you can use a twisting technique with the thumb and forefinger to remove the candle, or you can twist the candle off with a tweezers.

Remove the most vigorous candles first and wait until the others mature before heading them back. Pines can be so candled two or three times during a season. Such nipping encourages the next crop of needles to grow shorter and eliminates "spoke wheel" branch configuration. To stem growth completely, eliminate the entire candle.

If you want a branch to continue in length, remove all the candles except the one that grows in the direction you desire. Always allow three or four bundles of needles to remain after pinching most of the candle away. Each protrusion represents a needle cluster.

The most common mistake is to leave too much. Pinch young shoots just as needles begin to show. If you pinch too soon, you may get another crop of needles during the same growing season; if the needles have already sprouted, it is too late. If pines fail to become compact, candle-nipping probably was neglected—or it was not done at the proper time which is shortly after the candle emerges and before needle clusters show. If you have pines with "bottle brush" ends, this may be the reason.

Even after pinching at the proper time, some pines develop secondary buds or candles in the mid-summer. Select the buds you want to keep in order to extend the branch. Save one bottom and one side bud only to avoid spoke-wheel branches.

Removing pine candles, as in all pruning, may sap growth from the plant. Foliage manufactures food and passes it into the roots and trunk for storage. As long

PHOTO #23
Cedar elm, Ulmus crassifolia 'Nutt,'
23-inches tall, potted 1974 from collected material.

*Material collected from one hardiness zone and maintained in a different zone often does not respond the same as it did in the natural microclimate. While hardiness zones refer to cold temperature tolerances and can be adjusted with winter protection, prevailing microclimate controls growth habit. When the climate of maintenance differs from the climate of origin, there is bound to be some difference in growth response.*

*This elm was collected from Texas zone 7 and transferred to New York zone 6. The long, hot, dry summers and relentless sun exposure of Texas differ considerably from the short, temperate, humid summers of New York. While this Texas elm never responded with the luxurious foliage characteristic to the climate of geographic origin, the wispy growth, delicate branching fretwork and ramification are redeeming features.*

*Critically, the trunk is too slender for the tree height. While the tree was shortened with a surrogate terminal when first potted, additional reconstruction is necessary to bring it down to a more correct proportion. The graceful movement, however, outweighs this disadvantage.*

as pine species exhibit good vigor, candle pruning may be done each time new candles appear. Prudence suggests that newly-potted pines should not be candled until vigorous growth has become re-established.

**Elms.** Chinese elm, Catlin elm and Zelkova are the most popular varieties for bonsai. One native in the Southwest, *Ulmus Crassifolia* (Texas elm, see Photo #23), grows in high pH soils and has a gnarled and twisted trunk. Catlin elm is characterized by very small, shiny, dark green leaves and has the smallest leaves compared with other elms grown for bonsai. It is a sport of the common Chinese elm, *Ulmus parviflora* and, as such, it is not officially recognized as a distinct variety. It grows much slower than the Chinese elm and produces a finer network of twigs and branches.

All elms are vigorous growers. They respond to training and develop branch ramification in one or two growing seasons. While Chinese elms shed foliage in late autumn, Catlin elm often retains evergreen foliage during mild winters.

Elms in nature grow in the classic broom-style shape and lower branches become pendulous at the ends with rounded crowns. They respond noticeably to fertilizer and, when lacking nutrition, leaves quickly become thin and off color. Over-fertilizing results in larger leaf growth which defeats the main characteristics of the species. Heavily diluted soluble fertilizer (one-quarter to one-half strength) applied monthly from May through September will retain foliage size and provide adequate nutrition.

All elms are pruned in the same way: New growth should be trimmed back to one or two nodes during the growing season for compact specimens and twig ramification. The last bud on a branch should be pointed outward. Remove strong terminal shoots. Twigs growing inward or straight up should be removed unless they can be wired outward for styling improvement. Shoot trimming is a continuous summer procedure.

Elms are susceptible to infestation and should be sprayed against scale, aphid and caterpillar invasion once monthly from May through September. They also are particularly vulnerable to the fungus, black spot, and should be treated with a fungicide as soon as leaves appear in the spring—once monthly through the growing season and, again, when plants are placed away for winter.

**Weeping willow.** Cultivating the ubiquitous willow is easy to accomplish from cuttings in almost any month during the growing season. When started in spring, a creditable specimen can be attained by the end of summer. Since willow cuttings readily root, select a thick cutting one to two inches in diameter with ample branchlets. Plant deeply in a mixture of half and half peat moss and sand. Support the cutting with string around the training pot to keep the plant rigid until roots take over. Prune away unwanted branches and train those that are left by bending them downward once or twice a week. Ultimately, these branches will remain weeping if the ends are left unpruned. Unlike other bonsai species, a willow's beauty lies in length and pendulous characteristic of the branches, so tips should not be cut back during the growing season. The following spring, cut branches back to within an inch or two from the trunk to thicken the branches. Also resume the pendulous training by flexing the branches as new growth becomes apparent. Willows grow fast and, in no time at all, a weeping specimen with good ramification will result. It is important to realize that new willow growth does not have the weeping characteristic. The branches grow upward until the length and weight force them downward. The mechanical act of "flexing" the branches gently will accomplish the weeping configuration without wiring.

**Azalea.** The most popular variety of azalea used for bonsai is the Satsuki with its small leaves, resplendent color and superior blooms although Kurume and other common varieties can be developed for bonsai cultivation. Their strong root growth and buttressed trunks make azalea particularly desirable for root-over-rock and rock-clasping styles (see Photo Sequence #18).

Another good characteristic is azalea's habit to sprout from old wood. However, azalea is notoriously resistant to training by wire and it is a never-ending chore. Brittleness of the wood also makes wiring rather risky and broken branches during bending are common. Training is best accomplished with new growth while it is soft which often sprouts even after a branch has been considered dead. Bending and wiring is a little easier in the fall by allowing the plant to become almost wilted and keeping it drier than usual.

Azalea should always be pruned and trimmed after flowering. Four or more new shoots elongate at the terminal of each branch. Some shoots will also appear along the trunk and these should be rubbed off unless a new branch is desired at a particular point. The easiest method for pruning is to wait until the new shoots are fully extended. Then prune back to one set of leaves. After several weeks, new shoots again will appear at each terminal. These new shoots will be shorter because the internodes were reduced. Prune back again to one set of leaves. This should be done while the shoots are still tender. This pruning process extends throughout the growing season. If you want flower buds to set, do not trim after August 15th.

Blooms should be removed before they turn to seed in order to conserve plant vitality. Since seed pods develop quickly after flowering, it is best to trim the blooms before they discolor. After flowers fade, seed pods have already set.

In natural surroundings, azaleas have no need to "reach for the sun" since they thrive in shade under tall neighbors. They should be kept in dappled sun or exposed to morning sun only.

Azalea is a paradox. While the species require perfect drainage, they also must be maintained on the moist side. They thrive in humus-rich soil, so the potting mix should contain at least one-third peat moss which also keeps the medium on the acid side and helps to retain the moisture necessary for the species to flourish. This can be accomplished by using one-third each of peat moss, aggregate (Turface) and coarse sand, separately screened.

Azaleas become easily infested with lace bug which can damage a plant quickly and defoliate and discolor leaves. Frequent spraying with malathion is the easiest control procedure.

Feed with an acidifier fertilizer such as cottonseed meal or Hollytone right after flowering to encourage vegetative growth and, again, in the fall just before getting them ready for wintering.

**Yew (Taxus varieties).**    Two main cultivated species (English yew, T. Baccata and Japanese yew, T. cuspidata) are superior for bonsai. There are many other varieties and the differences between them lie in their growth habits which vary from prostrate, weeping and spreading to pyramidal and columner growth styles. They are easy to work with and develop graceful lines and thick, gnarled trunks and branches. (See Photo Sequence #24). Dead portions of yew are easily convertible to beautiful driftwood specimens and examples abound of yew utilizing this feature. Old, established specimens in gardens are especially coveted for bonsai cultivation.

Continuously during the growing season, finger pick new terminal growth leaving only a few needles. This will encourage new side shoots along the rest of the branch and growth will become more compact. Foliage may yellow when plants are exposed to full sun during July and August and they should be moved to partial shade or dappled sunlight.

**Junipers.**    Junipers have many different forms and growing habits from the upright pyramidal to the creeping styles with prostrate branching. All are trimmed the same way. During the initial training period (after styling), pinch off new growth from branch ends as the branches elongate. Junipers grow slowly, so this "training maneuver" may take some time after the initial potting and the opportunity for such pinching may present itself only two or three times during the first growing season.

As the juniper matures, more and more new growth will present itself for pinching until, finally, flat pads or "clouds" of compact foliage will develop and they are much to be admired (see Photo #14).

During this stage, junipers need steady pinching throughout the growing season. The central bud at each branch tip should be pinched away and this occupation can be endless but the results are striking. Use the fingers. Scissors will make tip ends brown. Trim with scissors at the back only.

In addition to this almost daily attention, branches should be thinned out in the spring and autumn by removing growth at internodes and the small twigs that invariably appear between areas of thick foliage. Branch tips overlapping like shingles should be trimmed so only one remains at the branch end. Branchlets growing beneath branches should also be removed. They will be shaded anyway. And juniper branches should be triangular when viewed from the top wherever possible.

**Juvenile growth.**    Old junipers, and especially varieties with scalelike or whipcord foliage (Shimpaku, Prostrata, California, Hollywood) are resistant to drastic pruning compared with junipers that grow needlelike foliage (Foemina, Procumbens) although some varieties bear two types of needles simultaneously (Eastern redcedar).

When old junipers with predominantly scale-like foliage are heavily fertilized, maintained in too much shade, over-watered or pruned drastically, existing scalelike foliage cannot manufacture nutrients in sufficient quantity to be transported where needed. As a result, these factors, or a combination of them, produce a mass of juvenile foliage—elongated needle-like growth that replaces the scalelike formations. (See Photo Sequence #22). This is nature's emergency measure—more leaf coverage quickly to compensate for the pruning loss.

As a defense mechanism, other species produce elongated growth and larger foliage to compensate for reduced foliage capability; juniper species, however, resort to juvenile growth to generate nourishment from sunlight.

It takes years to get rid of juvenile growth. Only after the proper balance between roots, foliage and nutrition is once again established will the needles eventually shorten and revert to the natural scale variety. What is more, an old juniper will develop two or three inches of juvenile growth in one season as a result of too much drastic pruning or fertilizing whereas conventional scalelike growth—the form to be desired—will reappear slowly with growth about one inch or less per year.

An old juniper, therefore, requires the most conservative pruning policy. Steel yourself against any impulse to prune away more than the barest minimum in one season. Immature foliage can almost always be avoided if drastic pruning is done only during active growth

## PHOTO SEQUENCE #24
Yew, Taxus sp.,
24-inches tall, potted 1982 from nursery stock.

*The terminal of this planting, still in process of training, has been encouraged to thicken through uninterrupted growth ("Before"). The after photo, one season later, shows the terminal somewhat improved. Several more training seasons will be required for a "finished" terminal appearance.*

**BEFORE**                                    **AFTER**

and, then, very conservatively—which means mostly tip pinching. The best time to repot juniper species is in summer during the active growing period. Junipers also require a slightly higher soil pH. Add a tablespoon of dolomitic lime to the potting soil and a teaspoonful once monthly during the growing season.

### Eastern Redcedar, Juniperus virginiana

The ubiquitous Eastern redcedar and the comparable Rocky Mountain juniper are vigorous growers, have interesting bark and possess ample branch structure. The species is seldom offered for sale at nurseries. They are available, like the California juniper, almost wholly through collecting from the wild.

Misnamed "cedar" by the early settlers in Virginia, the species grows extensively throughout the East and into the Midwest except in the extreme northern and southern states. It is described in horticultural texts as an "ornamental."

In its natural habitat, Eastern redcedar is a medium-sized spirelike or pyramidal conifer that grows 30 to 40 feet tall and reaches an age of 100 years or more. The wood is soft and it is used commercially for cabinets, cedar chests and fence posts. If you can remember the color and odor of a freshly sharpened pencil, you'll appreciate one of its additional uses.

The foliage is both scalelike and needled. Scales are about 1/16-inch long. The bark is reddish brown, thin, fibrous and shreddy and, in older specimens, it becomes very picturesque.

Because of the low branching habit and open growth characteristic, collected specimens have ample structure and are easily styled. One of the growth disadvantages, however, is the habit to sprout persistently at internodes. This growth, sometimes difficult to get at, can spoil the overall design and result in rank growth rather quickly. Since needles are sharp, the species also is difficult to wire and wired branches tend to revert to original shapes.

Perhaps the most welcome virtue of the species is its availability. Eastern redcedar is easy to collect from the wild although it develops long taproots which sometimes go down 18-inches or more.

**Suitability for bonsai.** Because Eastern redcedar is so easily procured from the wild in many different thicknesses and endures all kinds of abuse, including bare-root collecting, it is particularly adaptable to group plantings. Unfortunately, it is suitable—except in rare instances—for nothing else. The trunk formation of naturally-grown, untrained specimens is invariably "straight as a stick," except where the plantings pictured here were collected.

Through the courtesy of the Westchester County, New York Park Department, the author was permitted to collect Eastern redcedar at one of the county reservations. The tract in which they were growing originally was a hayfield.

The county acquired the property in 1925. Saplings growing in the field seeded from mature trees in the hedgerow. The field, however, had been mowed by farm tractors for more than a generation.

The plantings were never allowed to grow to maturity. Obscured by pasture grasses, the trunks ranged in thicknesses from one-inch to two-inches or more—artificially dwarfed through constant mowing and cropping, acquiring shapes and contortion that would have taken years to accomplish through bonsai techniques, if, indeed, they could have been so shaped at all.

Some of these naturally dwarfed specimens could have been twenty to thirty years old. When they started to grow above the field grasses, along came the tractor to mow the grass and, with it, the wild specimens that were naturally seeded. The trunks thickened out of proportion to their heights. Maturing, the trunks became curved and twisted. While they fattened, more configuration was added in marked contrast to the stick-straight characteristics of the species grown without outside interference.

As the tractors criss-crossed the field, trunks and branches that managed to grow above the field grass were pruned, too—and these became the basis of fretwork for branch ramification. (See Photo #25).

Pictured on the following pages are collected Eastern redcedar specimens in various stages after collecting and potting. While the species is far from ideal material due to its growth vigor, need for constant attention to grooming and the normally upright and uninteresting growth traits—the unusual environment in the field from which they were collected provided a treasure-trove of material for unusual styling potential.

**Boxwood varieties.** (See Photo Sequence #3). Buxus varieties grow densely with frequent trimming back. Unwanted growth can be pinched at any time. Outer shoots should be trimmed so inner shoots can get light and air, otherwise inner growth will yellow and die back. Trim shoots growing upward or inward or wire them straight out. Remove small tails that develop at the ends of branches.

Boxwood varieties differ in their ability to resist cold, so the popular Kingsville box should be kept in shade or dappled sun. Full sun causes foliage to discolor. The Kingsville variety also is a favorite for indoor cultivation after exposure to a period of cold weather, about thirty days. Keep in a cool, sunny room—not in direct sun. They thrive in both acid and lime-rich soils and they are vigorous growers when planted on rocks. They should be fed frequently with very dilute fertilizer so-

### Eastern redcedar, Juniperus virginiana

*All the trees pictured were collected in 1974 and 1975 from an abandoned hayfield. In order to control pasture grasses, the tract was mowed several times each season. This periodic growth interruption and zig-zag mowing pattern produced the contorted trunks.*

*Due to the development of deep taproots, prominent surface roots were lacking in most of the specimens collected, a characteristic which made the material less pleasing for single-tree stylings. The plants were superb, however, for group plantings. The species is fast-growing and requires constant pinching and trimming to maintain style and proportion.*

PHOTO #25

*The trunk in the specimen shown in the ground is two-inches in diameter at the base, concealed by pasture grasses to a depth of six-inches.*

PHOTO #26

*Collected plants in training pots where they were allowed to develop untrimmed before styling.*

Eastern redcedar, Juniperus virginiana

PHOTO #27

*The trunk in this specimen developed impressive thickness and taper in the ground, but lack of surface roots resulted in a disappointing single-tree planting. The obvious fault would have been less apparent in a group styling.*

PHOTO #28

*44-inches tall, 45-inches wide, a group planting on a granite slab potted in 1977. This planting has never been dismantled for root-pruning. Instead, about two-inches of soil was periodically removed from the edges and overgrown roots were severed, after which new soil was added. (see "Restoring Group Plantings," page 42).*

lutions. If overfed, leaves get larger. Since all buxus species produce a surge of new growth in early spring, an application of fertilizer in February will produce vigorous, new growth. Pot in a gritty soil.

**Spruce species.**    The buds of spruces open at various times on the same tree, often three or four weeks after first new growth is observed. Diligent pinching is necessary when the buds have swollen in order to attain compact, tidy growth and this should take place before the buds have fully opened. If the needles themselves are apparent, it is too late. Pull off the new shoot between thumb and forefinger without disturbing the full outside needles. If you pinch full growth, the needles will turn brown. If thicker foliage is desired in an area, new shoots should be left untouched. Spruces usually make only one spurt of growth during the growing season.

**Hinoki cypress.**    Pinch off new, green tips as they appear during the growing season. This is easily accomplished by grasping the fan between thumb and forefinger and plucking away until all new growth has been reduced. Hinoki cypress does not sprout from old wood where branches or branchlets have been removed. The branches, therefore, must be kept open with wire so light can penetrate inside and encourage continuous new growth on existing foliage.

**Flowering crabapple.**    There are more than 700 varieties and cultivars of the *Malus* species which includes apples and crabapples. Collected specimens often are gnarled and picturesque, especially when gathered from abandoned groves browsed by deer and cattle. They are adaptable to many soil compositions and temperature extremes. Due to dominant top growth, they can be styled with a rounded crown rather than a distinct terminal (see Photo #9).

*Malus* species are rapid growers and must be restrained in order to avoid spoiling the initial styling. This is especially disheartening when, in the spring, you have scrupulously exposed the gnarled branches so common among apples only to find, as the season progresses, that new foliage has obscured the most attractive features. The best time to plan the styling and remove unwanted branches is in late winter while the tree is completely defoliated and the branching is readily apparent.

In the spring, branches will grow vigorously. Prune only for shaping. In June or July, branches should be cut back drastically to restore the design potential. Trimming should be continued during the growing season. Late summer growth is more compact, internodes are shorter and emerging leaves are smaller. The branches can also be wired in July while they are still limber and can be positioned so they do not conceal the trunk. New shoots developing on the trunk can be preserved to enhance the design.

The close attention to trimming that apples require may sacrifice flower buds for the following season, but you will be rewarded with tidy, compact growth without obscuring the trunk and branch configuration which are among the most desirable features of this splendid bonsai material.

The best time to pot and repot the species is when new shoots are apparent in the early spring and after they have been exposed to the required cold period. Apples have a sensitive mechanism when breaking dormancy. They require about fifty cumulative days under 45°F. and many do not grow well in areas where winters are mild. For small specimens, an artificial cold period can be created in the refrigerator.

Occasionally, a crabapple will be brought out of protection too soon, exposed to unaccustomed light and high temperatures. If the weather turns sharply downward, growth will be suspended. The tree will return to dormancy and, from all appearances, it has stopped growing and appears to have been stricken. Because of the sudden environment change, the plant has returned to dormancy and may remain inactive for several more weeks, only to come back to life after the second dormancy period has been completed. When this occurs, do not force growth until outside temperature becomes more stable. Restore the protective environment until new growth resumes and avoid extreme sunlight and temperature until leaves have fully emerged and additional shoots are apparent.

With all their styling advantages and responsiveness, apples also have disadvantages, the most important being their susceptibility to infestation and disease. Among these are apple scab, cedar-apple rust, powdery mildew, fireblight and leaf spot—plus an array of insect problems. Unless the variety or cultivar is known to be disease-resistant, and only about 10% of the whole spectrum can be considered in this category, a regular spray schedule is necessary. This involves a dormant oil application in spring and weekly applications from the time new growth is observed right through the growing season at the end of August. A single formulation known as "Fruit Tree Spray" is specific for apple species. This spray contains one or two fungicides, an insecticide and a miticide. Infestations occur quickly, so applications every ten days are necessary, even before you observe the presence of insects.

Do not fertilize apples while in bloom. The blossoms will be aborted. Wait until fruit has formed.

**Maple varieties.**    Maples should be pinched according to the stage of development. To encourage branch thickness and short internodes, allow the branch to grow rank for a season or two. An untrimmed branch can grow as long as two feet during the growing season with corresponding thickness (see Photo Sequence #21). This will make the maple bonsai appear lop-sided for a while, but the results are worth it. Allow the branch to remain through the winter. The following spring, as new growth starts to emerge, cut the branch back to suitable length. If trimmed too soon, new growth will not break out as quickly. This procedure is especially effective low down on trunks where you want thicker branches.

For established maples, pinch only to limit growth. When the first set of leaves starts to unfold, pick out the next set that is starting to show on each branch or branchlet. If the central bud has already developed, nip the stem of each new leaf. This will develop side growth and result in a more mature-looking branch.

Trident maples are apical dominant and tend to produce bushy crowns at the expense of branches below. Failure to prune top growth hard enough deprives lower branches of growing vigor. Prune lower branches first; when they show signs of new growth, about two weeks later, then tackle the top. In this way, lower branches will have a head start to lengthen without interference by the top growth.

Trident maple leaves may scorch when kept in full sun during July and August. They should be displayed in partial shade during these months. While they need a moderate cold period during winter months, Trident maples should be protected against wind and sun.

For all maples, shoot-trimming is a continuous summer procedure and, since they are vigorous growers, wire imbeds into branches quickly—often as fast as three or four weeks after wiring. (For trunk characteristics, see "Trident Maple Tunnels," page 19).

# 7. *The Wiring Ritual*

Wiring is to bonsai what bricks and stone are to architecture, what color is to art, what vocabulary is to writing. Wiring is a bonsai styling *device* and, without it or other means of shaping, there can be no bonsai as we know the state of the art.

Most bonsai require wiring from the very beginning, even collected specimens, plus periodic refurbishment during the life span of the tree. When the fifty master bonsai specimens were presented by the Japanese to the United States as a Bicentennial gift in 1975, many in the collection had been cultivated for as long as 350 years. If any bonsai could have been considered "finished," it certainly would have been this superb group. Yet, many of the trees had been recently wired.

Most of the existing bonsai texts have abundantly detailed wiring techniques, wire gauges and bending procedures, so treatment of these phases will be confined to the basics. Here are the fundamentals:

1. When wiring two branches with one piece of wire, start at a junction and loop the wire below the crotch. Wire three or four turns on the first branch, go back and completely wire the second branch, then return and finish the first. This sequence firmly anchors the wire and avoids slippage.

2. When wiring a single branch, anchor the wire for an inch or two around the trunk or another branch. Looped wire around a single branch will not hold unless well anchored.

3. Wire at 45° angles and move your hand back toward the trunk at each turn to keep the wire snug.

4. Do not cross wires for appearance reasons.

5. There is no way to determine in advance the precise wire gauge that will hold. It is a matter of judgement. Branch flexibility depends on thickness and species. Usually, the wire should be about one-third the thickness of the member being wired when copper wire is used. For hard woods such as maple, the wire must be thicker. When aluminum wire is used, the wire gauge must also be increased.

   Always test the branch for bending before applying wire. Then test the wire. After a little practice, the correct gauge to use will become automatic.

   If a single wire is insufficient to hold the branch or trunk in position, do not remove. Add a second wire of the same gauge or thinner. Coil the second wire as close to the first wire as possible.

6. When coiling thin wire around a branch, leave a tail at the end for easy removal. Thick wire should be removed by cutting it off in links.

Despite the fact that wiring is an integral part of bonsai styling, we sometimes hear a bonsai enthusiast exclaim, "I don't believe in wiring; it makes a bonsai appear artificial and, besides, wiring could injure the branches. I want my trees to look natural."

This, as we know, is a distortion of the facts. The current wisdom is that wiring is used to embellish bonsai—to give it style and create an ideal. It cannot be considered "artificial" because it is a tool and the tool is removed once the function has been performed. The Japanese have given us the wiring procedure in order to shape our trees and make them bonsai. In fact, the Japanese have disciplined themselves to ignore the presence of wire on their bonsai. They see only the shapes that wire intended the branches to become.

As far as "branch injury" is concerned, if wire is coiled around a branch with a measure of discretion—not too loosely and not too tightly—and if it is removed before the wire cuts into the bark, the risk of blemishing the branch is minimal. A lot depends on the species, too—whether the wood is soft as in pines, or has the smooth bark and vigor of growth as in the willow which can become flawed from wire in thirty days or less. And, if we are alert, wire that has done its job should be removed before it scars the bark.

The objection, "I want my bonsai to look natural . . ." is a tacit admission that the practitioner fails to recognize the necessity for wiring. If one has not learned to wire bonsai, it is surprising how quickly the skill can be acquired. The few rules have to do with neatness so the wiring will be less conspicuous, plus the mechanics of forces that enable the wire to hold the member in the shape intended. This is *creation*—and it does require a modicum of skill. The more one wires bonsai, the more proficient one becomes.

Finally, without wiring, there can never be good bonsai—unless we choose to practice the Lingnan method of branch training introduced by the Chinese centuries ago, and which involves a "grow and clip" procedure wherein a branch is allowed to lengthen and expand for several growing seasons and then cut back to change direction (see page 64). It may take years to develop a beautiful bonsai with the Lingnan method but, then, our dubious hobbyist can exclaim, "Look, mom, no wire."

From the practical point of view, bonsai require wiring from the very beginning of the creative process, plus *continuous* wiring each season for as long as it takes for a specimen to reach perfection.

**Where to start.**    Always wire lower branches first. It stands to reason that thicker branches lower down will require greater stress forces for bending than lighter branches higher up and the lower branch configuration will determine positioning of the ones above. Since wires should never cross (an esthetic principle rather than a mechanical advantage) it is easier to apply thin wire parallel to a thicker one.

**When to wire.**    Juniper, pine and willow are the most flexible species. Maples, apples, quince and azaleas are more flexible when dormant. All branches are more likely to snap during wiring and bending when they are turgid, that is, when considerable moisture is present in plant tissues. Once the sap starts to flow, branches become brittle. Some growers avoid watering for several days before bending to allow branches to dry out. It stands to reason, however, that plants would have to dry out much longer than a few days to make much of a difference.

If you forget the flexibility rule, just think of a piece of celery which is brittle and fresh when full of moisture—limp and easy to manage when moisture is absent. It is also easier to wire deciduous species when there are no leaves to get in the way. You can avoid this by wiring before buds break and bending before new growth emerges.

February is the best month to wire deciduous species, but the procedure should be done outdoors to avoid stimulating new growth prematurely. When replaced outdoors to complete dormancy, new growth stimulated by indoor temperature may be winter-killed. The other option is to keep newly wired material indoors until frost risk has passed.

Ordinarily, wiring can be done at any time, but always avoid damage to tender buds even if an ample supply is available on a branch. Young buds rub off very easily. If there is any special time to avoid this, it would be to wire before buds appear in the spring or when new leaves are fully developed in the summer.

**When to avoid wiring.**    Green growth is never wired. Mere handling of fresh growth will damage it and, even if coiling wire around a green branch is successful, it will cut in quickly. Do not wire branches that show signs of stress. Bending or mere pressure of wire may interfere with the ability of the branch to transport moisture and a stressed branch, especially if it is an important one, needs as much help as possible.

**Wiring hazards.**    Bending a branch disturbs normal growth. On the upward side of a branch bent downward, the newly formed cells of sapwood are stretched; on the under side, they are compressed. This distortion retards new growth and if there is insufficient time during the growing season for the branch to recover, the branch may languish. Result: The branch may be shaped in a pleasing esthetic position, but you have altered the ability of the branch to perform its function for the tree as a whole. The solution: Wire when the branch is still dormant and before the first surge of spring growth.

**Wire damage.**    Some growers feel that marks left by wire add age or character to the appearance of bonsai. There is a line, however, between which blemishes add character, such as jin or calloused heartwood, and which result from careless grooming. While it is not uncommon to see wire cuts on bonsai grown in Japan, bonsai with such blemishes are never exhibited. This also depreciates the bonsai value and advanced growers are severely criticized for allowing wire cuts to develop.

Branches on maples and elms suffer wire damage quickly, often only two or three months after wire application. If the damage is severe, the blemish is always conspicuous. Juniper wire damage takes longer to develop because the species is so slow-growing. Younger specimens of all species are quick to show wire cuts. Older bonsai can sometimes go a year or more without blemishing the branches but it also takes longer for branches to stay trained.

Species with exfoliating bark such as corticosa elm or pine recover quickly and, if it is any consolation, all branches that have become spiraled with wire cuts will be permanently fixed in that position. If it becomes necessary to re-wire such branches, reverse the spiral direction or, if this is not possible, simply avoid the grooved areas. Needless to say, it will pay to keep all wired branches under close scrutiny.

Thin wire will cut into branches faster than thick wire because it usually is coiled around thin, new growth. Young branches thicken faster than old branches, so wire damage on new growth may become apparent after only a month or two. Also, thin wire cuts into bark faster because it is easier to coil around a branch than thicker wire and, since less effort is required, it goes on tighter.

**Back branch wiring.**    Do not neglect the back branch during the wiring procedure. There is a natural tendency to give the back branch less attention than other members because the back is not as carefully observed as the front. Adequate shaping of the back branch, however, can enhance the view from all positions. Raising or lowering the back branch slightly or fanning out the branchlets so they are more visible from the front will add depth and improve the overall impression. The back branch need not be too long. The mere suggestion of foliage refined by wiring at the back is sufficient.

**How to conceal blemishes through wiring.** The most important function of wiring is to communicate shape and movement, but deception is one of the requisites of the art, too. Thus, wiring can be used to shape a branch, to conceal a fault such as an unattractive bend in a trunk, a disfiguring scar, an uninteresting straight trunk—or any other portion of a tree that may leave something to be desired in the elements of design.

**Estimating wire lengths.** Few bonsai procedures are more frustrating than wiring a branch only to find a wire length too short before coming to the end of the branch. When this happens, there is no need to start over again. Just add another length of wire to the false end and continue wiring to the end of the branch. The best way to make sure a wire length is long enough is to wire from a coil rather than from a single length although this is not always practical. Another way is to cut a length of wire double the length of the branch up to branches one-quarter inch thick. Increase the wire length for each one-sixteenth inch of branch thickness beyond a quarter-inch. If a double strand of wire will be used for one branch, double the foregoing estimate. It is better to over-estimate the length of wire required. You may waste a few inches of wire here and there, but the time saved will more than compensate.

**Wiring caution.** When wiring a single branch, the usual procedure is to loop the wire around the branch or trunk as an anchor. Once the wire is so looped, hold it tightly with thumb and forefinger to avoid movement when continuing the spiral. If the loop is revolved around soft bark, the branch may be girdled and ultimately lost.

**Tied down branches.** Some growers attempt to train branches by tying them down to the pot or to a surface root. This practice seldom provides the correct branch shape from the trunk which is straight out and downward with the tip pointed upward. What generally results from a tied-down branch is an unattractive U shape. Also, if a heavy branch is tied down to one side of the container, the force may dislodge the rootball from the pot, unless the tree is also tied down on the opposite side to neutralize the force.

**Branch-training timing.** Conifers are the most resistant species to shape by wiring and require the longest time for branches to be trained to the point where they will hold the position. Generally, conifers take about a year or longer whereas deciduous species become "fixed" in a matter of months depending on the branch thickness. Also, conifers have a tendency to grow back to their original positions even after it appears as if they are permanently shaped, so wiring will have to be repeated again and again.

**Broken branch repair.** When a branch snaps during wiring, bend the branch back to its original position and leave the wire in place. If part of the cambium layer is still connected, the branch will recover, but it should never be wired again. It will only snap in the same place and, next time, it will be finished. Branches that continue to grow after breaking do not "graft" themselves as many suspect. Instead, the broken ends callus over and compartmentalize in the same manner as a large branch severed from the trunk. The connected portion takes over the job of supplying moisture and nutrition. No matter how thick the broken branch eventually grows, it is only the connected portion that fulfills this function.

**Winterizing and wire.** Wire should be removed before trees are wintered. The theory has been advanced that more cold is conducted to the branch through the metal compared with exposure to the air. Not so. Wire should be removed before wintering because it may bite in on fast growing species such as maples. Also, it is important to inspect group plantings for wire cuts before the wire becomes hidden by foliage. After the trees in a group planting develop, it is more difficult to get in and around and, in so doing, branches may be broken.

**Annealing wire.** Annealing not only makes wire easier to bend, but the process also removes the shiny copper surface which many find offensive. If you choose to use wire not annealed but object to the conspicuous appearance, simply coat the wire, after application, with lime-sulphur solution (Orthorex). Use a small brush. If untreated, however, the shiny copper appearance will eventually become weathered and unobtrusive.

To anneal short lengths of wire (up to two feet long) simply straighten the wire and hold it over a gas burner on the kitchen stove until it is cherry red. Use a pliers. Coiled wire can be annealed in an outdoor charcoal burner. If left on red hot coals for more than an hour, however, the wire may become brittle rather than flexible. Thicker wire (No. 6 or No. 10) can be left to heat for a longer period of time and may require up to an hour to become properly annealed.

**What annealing does.** Heating copper wire changes the shape of the crystalline structure and softens it as long as the crystals remain in the same position. When the wire is bent, however, some crystals revert to the original positions and the wire becomes hard again. Wire that is re-used is never as soft as it was when first annealed, but neither is it quite as hard as the original state. It is a nuisance to straighten wire for re-use, but short lengths should be saved for emergencies.

**Aluminum wire.**   This material is soft and requires no annealing. Thicker wire, however, is necessary to accomplish the same bending efficiency as copper wire. About twice the thickness of copper wire is necessary when aluminum wire is used, or apply a second wire to the branch to hold it in the desired shape.

**Removing insulation.**   If you use copper wire covered with insulation, a quick way to remove the covering is to lay it on a concrete walk or a brick and tap lightly with a hammer, just enough to crush the insulation. Another easy method is to secure one end of the wire in a vise. Hold the other end of the wire tightly and, with a utility knife, peel away several inches of the covering. The rest of the insulation can be removed with the fingers. Don't try to burn the insulation off. It's messy and the fumes from burning plastic may be toxic.

**Removing wire.**   Thick wire should be removed by cutting it into links with a bonsai wire cutter made for this purpose rather than trying to unwind it. After heavy wire is twisted around a branch, it loses the softness that was provided by the annealing process. If you try to unwind hardened wire, you may damage the bark and damaging the bark of a branch full circle is the same as a girdle—fatal. Thin wire, on the other hand, is more easily removed by untwisting. If a wire cutter is used in this situation, you risk severing a branch, too. Tuck in the wire end as you unwind thin wire or cut it off so it won't flop around. It can become entangled in an adjacent branch, damage it, or defoliate a branch without your realizing it.

To remove wire embedded in the wood, hold the branch with the fingers and lift up an end with a small blade or thin-nosed pliers. Then unwind the wire while holding the branch securely with your fingers. It is impossible to remove wire in links when it bites into the bark.

**Trunk bending tip.**   Spray the bark with water after wiring and before bending to help avoid cracking the bark. While tissues within are more flexible when dry, moisture on the bark protects it against splitting.

**Lost branch.**   When a branch dies after wiring, a close inspection may reveal that careless bending may have caused it to snap. This may not have been apparent during the wiring and bending procedure because the wire deceptively held the branch in place.

**Straightening wire.**   Coiled wire up to size 16 or 18 can be straightened by grasping each end with a pliers and pulling sharply. One end can also be fixed in a vise and the other end yanked hard. Thicker wire can be straightened by pulling it over a round wood or metal object such as a post.

**Save tire weights.**   Various spruce species have the unfortunate ability to spring back almost to their original positions after wires are removed. A good way to hold these stubborn branches and branchlets in position is to use small pieces of lead tire weights suspended by wire from the undersides. The weights are inconspicuous and needle growth soon obscures them even more. The weights can be cut with a hacksaw. Almost any garage or tire shop will let you have a few discarded weights, no charge, or new ones can be purchased inexpensively.

**Wiring and pinching.**   After wire is removed, branch tips should be pinched periodically. The tips of branches, especially junipers, reach upward toward the sun. The rest of the branch follows that direction. As the branch grows longer, it will continue to bend upward, tending to revert to its original position, defeating the wiring purpose in the first place. Except for branches bent downward by their own weight, all branches have a tendency to "reach for the sun." To retain the style and terminal positions, major branches must be re-wired from time to time.

**Wiring refresher.**   Wiring bonsai is strictly an esthetic requisite. How you want the trunk and branches to be shaped is a matter of your artistic sense. Once the technique of wiring is mastered, the rest is pure art.

The most neglected of all grooming procedures, however, is the fine wiring procedure. Resist the temptation to prune away a small branch that can be wired into the plane just because the fine wiring ritual is tedious. While this procedure is time-consuming, it is absolutely necessary if you want a finished bonsai. Pay particular attention to fine wiring of the apex. This is the key focal point where the eye comes to rest after observing the roots, trunk and branches.

Another tedious procedure is fanning out the branches at the ends. Look at the junipers growing along the roadways and silhouetted against the sky. The ends of the branches are always splayed outward in the same plane to get more sunlight. Wiring the branch ends in this fashion pays dividends in attractive configuration. Remember, wiring has two purposes: To help attain an ideal form and correct overlapping branches for better sun exposure.

# 8. *Containers*

Choosing the proper container requires a measure of skill, not only from the standpoint of plant health and vigor, but also from the standpoint of esthetics. The pot should contribute to the harmony of the presentation as a frame to a picture. Simple shapes, in order to refrain from detracting from the main object which is bonsai, are best.

There are considerable differences of opinion, as in any art form, as to which of the hundreds of different styles of pots go best with the different styles of bonsai and opinions are based largely on personal taste rather than strict rules of design. Certain obvious elements, however, should be kept in mind when making pot selections.

Bright colors or garish pots can overwhelm the bonsai while terra cotta red pots as well as the standard earth-color containers are quite suitable for coniferous species. Brightly-colored pots, even pure white, should be used discreetly unless flowers or berries are to be emphasized in which case they should present a contrast. Remember, however, that flowers and fruit occupy only a small percentage of the time a bonsai is viewed.

One school of thought holds that the width of the pot should be equal to approximately two-thirds the height of the tree if this is the largest dimension or two-thirds of the branch spread if the bonsai is wider than it is tall. For thick-trunked bonsai (two inches or more in diameter) the depth of the pot should be approximately the same thickness as the trunk.

Another school contends that the length of the pot *plus* the depth should equal the greatest dimension, height or width. Ideally, the pot depth should be about the same as the trunk thickness at the soil line except for thin-trunked bonsai. For trunks one-half inch in diameter or less, it would be impractical to contemplate a pot ½-inch deep for a single planting although wide, shallow pots are ideal for group plantings. For thin-trunked bonsai, select a pot in proportion to the plant, disregarding the depth. It's a visual *mass* of the whole that becomes the criterion. If the overall appearance looks comfortable to the eye and is harmonious, this will convey the correct impression.

Certain bonsai styles are natural for specific pot configurations but, here again, there are no fixed rules. Taste and harmony govern the considerations.

For example, some pots are graceful and delicate in structure and would never do for a masculine, heavily-muscled trunk while whispy, graceful branch contours suggest lipped pots and smooth curves. Severe rectangular containers go well with formal upright bonsai; lipped containers harmonize with informal upright and slanting styles.

On the other hand, it stands to reason that a heavily gnarled bonsai such as a flowering crabapple with a prominent trunk, surface roots and marked buttress, should be potted in a container of the plainest design in order to provide a severe contrast and allow the beautiful characteristics of the bonsai to dominate completely. Tall trees and slender trunks characterized by the literati or bunjin style belong in dish-shaped containers and a windswept style seems to demand a long, shallow container to emphasize direction of the wind and tree movement.

Remember, oversize pots for young plant material can be harmful because too much soil prevents the medium from drying out. Soils that remain too wet for too long can prevent root development. Undeveloped root masses will not grow into sodden soils. Those who planted cuttings in large pots and which failed to take could attribute the failure to overpotting.

**Mending broken pots.** Containers that have fallen off benches or tables and smashed to smithereens against cement or rocks below are impossible to restore. But pots cracked or broken into two or three pieces through freezing or simple breakage are easy to assemble and the deception may barely be noticed.

If there are more than two or three pieces, forget it. They will never fit together cleanly unless you are a restoration expert because even the slightest amount of cement will alter the articulation and render the process useless. Simple breaks, however, can be joined together very successfully.

Containers that have been mended can be used as training pots, or the restored portion can be made unnoticeable by placing that portion in the back or other location where it is less apparent. The procedure for restoring a two or three piece break and making the pot waterproof is easy.

First, fit the pieces together carefully to make certain

the outside of the pot is in practical condition to restore. Inside chips make no difference. When fitting the pieces, be careful not to chip away any of the outside edges.

When you are certain the pieces can be properly fitted, use DuPont cellulose cement to glue them together. Join the pieces in rapid succession without waiting for the cement to harden or dry. There is enough latitude in the setting time of cellulose cement to shift the pieces for perfect articulation. The celluose cement is used merely to hold the pieces together until the restoration can be finished and the slow setting time of cellulose allows for perfect positioning. Anyone who has had experience mending china knows how important that is.

After the cellulose cement is applied and the parts are in alignment, apply pressure with your hands to join the pieces as closely as possible. After a few minutes, secure the assembly with rubber bands or string and let the joints dry and harden overnight. Any surplus cement on the outer surfaces can be removed with a blade at the very end.

Remember, cellulose cement is not waterproof. The purpose is merely to hold the pieces together until the inside of the pot can be worked on to create a waterproof joint.

Waterproofing the inside of the pot is done with epoxy packing such as Duro epoxy cement and filler made by Loctite Corporation. This is a two-part packing that creates a water-tight, stone hard finish. Don't bother to remove any cellulose accumulation from the inside of the pot. Cover the entire length of the crack with a bead of epoxy packing about one-quarter inch wide. Bring the bead to within one-half inch from the top of the pot so it will not be noticeable when the pot contains soil. The epoxy packing will render the inside of the pot waterproof making it usable for bonsai and, chances are, the pot will never break again in the same place.

Obviously, pots that have been mended should not be used for public exhibit if there is any trace of reconstruction, but pots mended as described are perfectly usable for training or housing material subject to less discriminating observation.

**Training pots.**    Clay azalea pots are the best substitute for expensive ceramic pots. They are relatively inexpensive, they have good proportions and they have drainage holes which low-cost plastic pots lack. It is possible, however, to create holes in plastic pots with a conventional drill or by burning a hole with a red hot iron rod or screwdriver—outdoors, of course. Soil dries faster in clay pots than plastic varieties.

# 9. *Moss and Lichen*

According to the New York State Conservation Department, over 450 varieties of moss and lichen grow in New York State alone. When you multiply this by the numerous varieties that flourish in other parts of the country, the total reaches into the thousands.

Mosses are spore growers whereas lichens are plants consisting of algae and fungi growing in close association with each other to form a perfect example of symbiosis—different organisms joining for their mutual benefit. While each of the organisms can be separated and grown on its own, the individual growths will look nothing like what they formed together, lichen.

**Browsing for moss and lichen.** It is easy to locate a dozen or more varieties by inspecting your own backyard or nearby woods. Look at the bases of trees and shady areas—on walkways, sidewalks and brick walls. You will find moss spores in abundance or the start of colonies in the suitable environments. Look on the bark of trees, old stumps and rocks. These are the lichens. Mosses and lichens may look alike, but they are specialists and they flourish under widely different conditions.

**How to use it on your bonsai.** A touch of moss and lichen here and there on trunks and branches and prudently distributed over the soil surface does wonders to create the illusion of age. Surface roots can be emphasized by tastefully outlining them with fine moss or lichen. Lichen does not spread as rapidly as moss, but it will look more natural and immediately communicate a venerable atmosphere.

Both moss and lichen are easy to transplant. Moss can be lifted from the ground with a trowel or knife blade. Scrape off as much soil as possible from the back, moisten in water and press on the soil surface. For moss and lichen growing on tree trunks or rocks, scrape off a piece with a small pen knife blade and carefully carry it to your bonsai. Press it on the soil surface without touching it with your fingers which may alter its delicate pH. Do this several times to establish different colonies.

For the most pleasing and natural effect, moss and lichen should be spread around in random patches to simulate the way it grows in nature. Then sift small amounts of fine soil over the edges and between pieces. Unless a planting is mounded on a slab or grown on a rock and ground cover is used to keep the soil from washing away, moss should be used sparingly. Never cover the entire soil area with moss to imitate a Mount Vernon lawn.

**Applying lichen to trunks.** Colonies of lichen can be encouraged to grow on trunks, especially if there are bark excrescences or plates like the bark of Ponderosa pine and five-needle pine. With the blade of a pen knife, lift off small quantities of lichen from existing colonies growing on tree trunks, fences or shelf edges on the display bench. Do not scrape off the lichen as it will blow away before you have a chance to transfer it. Carefully implant the lichen on several spots of the new host. If you can't get the lichen to stay on the surface, press it into the fissure. Some areas will take and expand into new colonies to give the trunk a weathered and ancient appearance.

**It's not moss.** Beware that small star-shaped growth on soil surfaces many think is moss, but is not moss at all—it's a plant, liverwort. If you don't keep after this pest, it will take over the soil surface and also take forever to eradicate. Liverworts also occur as long, chain-like growths. They are attractive at first, but soon proliferate.

The only way to eliminate the rascals is to carry a tweezer in your pocket. Every time you go out to spend a few minutes with your bonsai, use the tweezer. A touch of vinegar with a cotton swab will get rid of an occasional out-cropping, but too much of this may alter the soil pH.

If we are not selective, some true mosses can get out of hand, too. That is why moss on soil surfaces should never be allowed to grow rampant. Tightly-packed moss could slow down water percolation through the soil and impede air circulation. Excessive moss over the soil surface can also deceive your observation to determine when the soil surface is dry. If moss becomes rampant, it may be necessary to scrape all of it from the soil surface, re-dress the surface with new soil and start the moss planting over again.

**Browning moss.**  It's a good sign when moss discolors during the hot months of July and August. Since moss needs moisture, it means the bonsai's water requirement apparatus is working well. Discolored moss will restore itself when cool weather returns and moisture requirements of the bonsai are in balance with the soil.

**Cultivating ground covers.**  To develop a bed of moss and lichen, spread cheesecloth over a planting flat containing 50% each peat moss and sand. Take clumps of moss and lichen and pulverize. A blender will do.

Then spread the powdered mixture over the moistened bed, keep moist and store in the shade.

**Mossing rock plantings.**  When applying moss or lichen to rocks, use U-shaped wire anchors to retain the patches. These anchors will hold the moss until you can wrap the planting with one-inch gauze bandage to contain the moss covering until it becomes established. The bandage will rot away in three or four weeks and, by that time, you will have an attractive, sturdy mossy covering. The narrow gauze bandage is easier to handle than cheese cloth.

# 10. *The Watering Dilemma*

The bonsai artform is replete with contradictions. This is apparent in advice about fertilizing, soil mixes and amendments, potting with dry vs. moistened soil, soil pH—even the very definition of bonsai has had many interpretations by practitioners of the art, some allegorical and others literal.

When the author was first introduced to bonsai in 1965 and the potting ritual became the all-consuming dictum of life or death for the budding masterpiece, coarse material for the bottom soil was gospel. This was supposed to guarantee drainage. No longer. Now the leading authorities caution against the use of coarse soil on the bottom based on the theory that it actually tends to accumulate water due to the varying soil interfaces.

Then there was the question of pruning paint. All cuts had to be "bandaged" with black tar-like sealer to thwart infestation and disease. No more. Now the theory holds that wounds heal themselves. Once a branch is cut, the wound "seals itself" to contain the injury and prevent rot from spreading throughout the trunk.

In addition, the pruning process, itself, has been reversed by the academicians who now state that, for trees growing in nature, pruning should be accomplished not as close to the trunk as possible, but outside the branch "collar" which is the source of a healing hormone. Of course, in bonsai the esthetic consideration is paramount, so we use concave pruners to conceal the blemish as much as possible—and it does heal.

The controversy of light vs. darkness for wintering bonsai still goes on, although a compromise has been reached wherein bonsai wintered below freezing need no light, whereas those not fully dormant do need some light to retain vigor.

Even the masters on the national scene are sometimes diametrically opposite in their theories on care and culture which doubtless means that all are correct and that sometimes it makes no difference. In bonsai styling, differences of opinion are marked by contrast depending on the geographical area, background or ethnic influence and the measure of art training or education one may have had, although the history of art and architecture is loaded with examples that originally were in dispute only to have survived as masterpieces.

**Facts of life.** Four things are vital for any plant to grow and flourish—light, nutrition, air and water. All these topics have been subjected to disparity among the bonsai community, but the area of watering takes the prize when it comes to differences of opinion, instruction and procedure. One reason for the variance, perhaps, is that *overwatering* in bonsai may be one prime cause for stress and gradual decline although it is often the element least attributed to plant loss. In contrast, when plants are dry, the demise is fast and the reason is readily apparent; when overwatering is the culprit, the plant slowly fails. It may take a full season to suspect something is wrong.

A small faction of hobbyists insists that watering should always be done with a Japanese watering can from high above to simulate rain, others caution against using a coarse hose nozzle—or watering in the sun and never after dark—or using runoff rain water exclusively which is understandable in areas where water use is limited or treatment factors contaminate the supply.

Kyuzo Murata,[7] a famous Japanese master, once exclaimed in one of his most lyrical admonitions that the act of watering bonsai symbolizes the outpouring of love. Who can deny the exultant feeling of satisfaction one experiences when a dry bonsai pot is soaked and the foliage takes on a lifelike sheen and appearance, even if the observation merely represents the reflection of more light from the surfaces of moistened leaves?

**The timing factors.** The most important schism in the watering mystique, however, is the dichotomy about *when* to water. One school holds that bonsai soil must always be somewhat moist; others respond that the soil surface should always be *dry* before the pot is watered at all and, at the same time, the soil should be soaked thoroughly so the water runs through the drainage hole.

Actually, a pot that appears to be dry on the surface can be adequately moist in the soil below. Make this simple test: Observe a bonsai that had been watered only when the soil surface appeared dry. Before watering again, lift the planting out of the pot. Notice that the soil below the top half-inch will be moist, and sufficiently so to sustain the plant for some little time because surface evaporation, due to insulation of the upper surface by dry soil, is virtually eliminated. Every bonsai doesn't have to be watered each time you reach for the hose or watering can. A period of dryness is what the roots require in order for air to penetrate the soil mass. A few extra hours of soil dryness will do no harm.

The soil of bonsai kept in full sun all day will dry out twice as fast as specimens maintained in partial sun (four or five hours a day) or dappled sun. Naturally, small pots dry out faster than large ones and very small pots, four inches across or less, should not be exposed to full sun at all.

As mentioned above, bonsai can go for a considerable period on the "dry" side. Plants in nature are programmed to resist drought during periods of insufficient rainfall. Notice what happens to the leaves of broadleaf species in the ground (rhododendrun, ilex, pieris, azalea) when rainfall is sparse: the leaves curl, as they do during cold weather, to close the stomata that transpire moisture. During periods of heavy rain, on the other hand, plants in nature do not "drown" because a network of tubelike passageways go from the upper layers down to the water table below to create drainage.

**The daily watering regimen.** In contrast to nature, the micro-environment of bonsai would naturally dictate time limits of dryness in hours rather than days or weeks for specimens in natural surroundings. And in periods of heavy rain, it may not be necessary to water bonsai for several days thereafter. Most bonsai species have a wide tolerance between the two extremes of moist and dry. During hot, dry periods, however, it may be necessary to water twice a day—once lightly to supply humidity, then thoroughly later on.

In general, and in the experience of this author, there should be a dry period between waterings for a time interval depending on the pot size, soil drainage capability, sun exposure and species. With synthetic soils, however, this may be deceptive because drainage and surface evaporation become greatly improved. It is better to poke a finger down into the soil about half-an-inch when synthetic amendments are used to check the moisture below. If the soil feels damp, do not water.

Exceptions to the foregoing are bonsai in shallow containers and rock plantings using some peat muck in combination with surface moss as the growing medium. Also, bonsai on rock slabs do not retain moisture as effectively as those in pots. In these plantings, the soil must never dry out completely as peat muck will harden and take forever to restore. They require more frequent watering than bonsai in conventional containers, especially during the hot months of summer. Also, since there is very little nutrition value in muck, rock plantings should be fertilized more frequently than potted trees.

When evaluating moisture, foliage spraying may deceive your observation. Don't mistake foliage spray that falls on the soil surface for a truly moistened root ball. If you spray the *foliage* when the soil is dry at the surface, water thoroughly, as well.

Juniper, pine, spruce and other conifers are drought resistant and can endure longer periods without watering than the broadleaf or deciduous species. Watering any species when not needed will produce long internodes and weak color. Evergreen species such as azalea and Kingsville box must have good drainage and also be maintained on the moist side most of the time. At the other end of the spectrum are such species as bald cypress, semi-tropical species and willow which thrive in sodden soil.

These "rules and regulations" apply essentially for bonsai kept outdoors during the summer. For indoor environment, there are other requirements.

**The moisture compromise.** Much of the ambivalence about watering can be cleared up if we regard *moist* as halfway between *saturation* and *completely dry*. The object would be to maintain the soil between *saturated* and *moist* for the moist period and midway between *moist* and *completely dry* for the dry period. On a scale of zero to ten from completely dry to saturated, the ideal would be to maintain soils at 2.5 for the dry cycle and 7.5 for the moist period.

Potbound bonsai dry out faster than roots contained within a normal root ball with a soil buffer and may require watering two or three times a day. Newly-potted bonsai, on the other hand, demand very little water— perhaps a cupfull at a time—until transpiration is restored and new growth is evident. Overwatering newly-potted bonsai, generously root-pruned, except at the initial potting to settle the soil, is a frequent cause of failure.

Deciduous and broadleaf species cannot tolerate dryness too long, nor do they mind being kept on the moist side. Also, during periods of high humidity, soils do not dry out as fast in contrast to the drying effect of low humidity and brisk wind. Each situation requires individual evaluation, which we can do more or less automatically, depending on the species, container size, extent of top growth and weather conditions.

When soil is altered after potting, the new soil may have different drainage characteristics than that around the root ball. If you water for the new soil, the root ball containing the old soil may become sodden. Check the root ball, not the soil around the edges, until new roots reach out into the new medium.

If the soil surface fails to dry out between waterings, however, something is wrong. Either, (1) the soil lacks adequate drainage, (2) the plant receives too little sun, or (3) a pathological condition or infestation exists. Determine the limiting factor. Drainage and light exposure can be corrected; a plant declining for a host of other reasons is another matter.

**What is "Overwatering?"** Then there is the admonition about "overwatering". Is "overwatering" the application of too much water by *quantity* (at one time) or too much by *frequency* (too often)? If the soil construction is suitable, neither situation can prevail. If drainage is good, you can water until you are blue in the face and the excess water will harmlessly drain away. And if you water only when the soil surface is dry, the "frequency" aspects of overwatering don't exist at all.

The ideal soil environment contains enough coarse material to allow water to become "vapor" (see *Soils*, page 51). Standing water is destructive to fibrous roots. Only through "vapor" can the capillary roots perform their function for survival of the plant.

**The rationale.** In order to bring this critical phenomenon into focus, imagine creating a potting medium which discards "useless" water and retains capillary moisture that feeder roots can use. Just visualize a pot-full of ordinary marbles wherein each marble represents a unit of soil, sand, Turface or whatever. When water is applied to this mythical medium, it gushes out through the holes on the bottom of the pot.

As the water drains out, air goes in. On its way out, a slight film of water coats each marble. The water is held on the marble surface through "adhesion." As this water comes in contact with the air between the marbles, the water is transformed into "vapor"—because "vapor" is a mixture of water and air. It is the "vapor" which the hair roots absorb. "Free water" is useless to the plant.

Now, suppose we add to this mass of marbles a quantity of fine material such as fine sand or silt. In the beginning, this extraneous matter will stay at the top and there will be very little difference in the atmosphere in the marbles below it. After a while, the fine matter will work its way down between the marbles, the air spaces gradually disappear and the marbles become surrounded not with air, but with solid matter.

As we know, no two objects can occupy the same space at the same time. So when soil compacts through the introduction of fine materials, the first thing to be pushed out is the *air* and air contains oxygen which the plant needs for survival.

The bonsai may survive with rootlets in this sodden environment for some little time. In nature, nothing ever happens before your very eyes. But the roots, in a medium of free water, will struggle to survive and function—and gradually the root mass will stress and eventually decline—and so will the top.

In summary, good soil construction involves screening out the fine particles that may reduce air space—use coarse materials that will *create* air space—avoid the use of peat moss unless you have to—and, remember, the object in doing these things is to create perfect drainage. When you create perfect drainage, you don't

have to worry about overwatering—and when you don't have to worry about overwatering, you have eliminated the "Watering Mystique"—and you will know it in the physical response of your bonsai.

Finally, in the deep recesses of my memory I recall reading about the remarks of a Japanese master who claimed that it takes seven years to learn to water properly. Maybe this is the real mystique after all—but it has taken this grower more than seven years to discover that the real mystique lies not in the physical act of watering, but in applying water and getting rid of it at the same time.

**Watering mechanics.** It takes time to learn the characteristics of soil in a pot. To water properly, the soil must be soaked through from top to bottom until it is obviously draining away. Trouble occurs when we read instructions, "Keep the soil moist to the touch." Many novices interpret this by adding little sips of water to the pots every day. This keeps the soil "moist to the touch"—on the top. The bottom may be dry or almost so. In addition to the "feel" of moist soil, it also smells "woodsy." There is a sheen on the surface and moist soil is darker in color at the surface than dry soil.

It actually is unnecessary to touch the soil surface of each pot at watering time to evaluate moisture. Daily appraisal becomes automatic. After a little experience and observation, you will be able to determine which pots to water and which to pass.

When soil surface appears dry, water three times thoroughly—or until you observe water dripping from the drainage holes. When pots are kept on benches, it is difficult to observe whether water actually is draining away. Watering three times will guarantee thorough soil saturation. Water both sides of the bonsai, front and back. One-sided watering usually leaves the opposite side unsaturated.

**Species variations.** Different species of plants reflect sub-soil dryness in different ways. In the case of maple and azalea species, the leaves droop; in junipers and spruce, the needles turn yellow.

If you observe one of these symptoms and they disappear after a prolonged period of rain, you may suspect that you are not watering thoroughly enough. During periods of high temperature and high humidity, the soil does not dry out as fast. If the temperature is high and the humidity is low, soils dry quickly; if the temperature is high and accompanied with drying wind, you may have to water twice a day.

Soils in pots should never be kept wet for long periods except when it is unavoidable due to rain. Likewise, and regardless of the species, most bonsai will not tolerate a bone dry situation throughout the soil mass for long. Only cacti will endure this environment. Good drainage will minimize the risk of excessive rainfall; vigilance will reduce the risk of dehydration.

It is not unusual for some growers to bring plants under cover during long periods of rainfall and the story is told of one individual living in the East who subscribed to the local newspaper which circulated in the vicinity of the Tehachapi mountains in Southern California. When the newspaper reported rain in that desert area from which the grower's California juniper was collected, the bonsai was watered. This is a far-fetched example, but it illustrates the mystique with which many hobbyists view the watering ritual.

**Wholesome neglect.**   With great reluctance, the author has followed the practice of watering thoroughly only after soil surfaces in some fifty bonsai are obviously dry. If soil surfaces are not dry at watering time, the pots are passed until the next day. A collected Ponderosa pine maintained in full sun for fifteen years with a summer watering schedule of every-other-day has thrived and prospered. Wholesome neglect, when it comes to watering, is good for bonsai.

**Bonsai vs. houseplant watering.**   Growers accustomed to caring for houseplants find it difficult to make the transition to bonsai watering. Bonsai species usually are those that thrive in natural, temperate field conditions. Most houseplants are tropicals derived from areas of moist, high-humidity environments. Moisture requirements for the two areas of container-grown culture are opposite. Houseplants need more watering. In addition, houseplants kept indoors are exposed to relatively dry air conditions compared with bonsai kept outdoors.

**Watering and growth rate.**   Plants take up water as a function of metabolism. The more sunlight, the more active the metabolic rate. When moved to a shady location, a plant's need for water also is reduced. If sun-loving species (pine, juniper, other conifers) are left in shade too long, new growth becomes spindly.

Requirements for water also diminish during humid weather. If there is more moisture in the air, the plant will need less at the roots. Watering becomes less critical during spells of high humidity.

**Calculated risk.**   It probably isn't always necessary to leave your trees with a bonsai sitter when you go away for a few days. If bonsai are kept in partial shade, you are on safer ground. Even in the heat of summer, however, most bonsai species will tolerate two or three days of dryness. This treatment is not recommended on a frequent basis, but if pots are thoroughly watered before departure, an occasional lapse apparently does no harm.

**A choice of evils.**   When leaving bonsai unattended for two or three days and you are in a dilemma as to whether to (a) connect an automatic watering system, (b) engage a watering "sitter," or, (c) depend on a possible rainstorm to do the job, the choice should be either (a) or (b). Don't bank on the weather. Temporary over-watering will do no harm for a few days. Allow the soils to dry completely when watering is resumed. Conversely, if soils become bone dry for even a short period of time, the consequences may be fatal to many species. The risk of over-watering is much less than the risk of dehydration which is irreversible.

**Deep pot watering.**   When watering cascade plantings in deep pots, water them once. Then water the rest of the bonsai. Return to the cascades and water again—then a third time. Deep pots need three watering passes to saturate the soil. A deep container also has a tendency to hold water longer than shallow pots which is a common cause of root rot in cypress and yew species. The root rot is caused by high temperatures and free water around the roots. Perfect drainage is the solution.

**Watering in the rain.**   While a slow, steady rain will do a thorough watering job, a passing thunder shower may not provide the moisture you may think the pots are getting. A quick pass-over with the hose after a short rain will complete the job. Also, dense foliage in the crown of many bonsai may serve as an umbrella and prevent light rain from saturating the soil beneath the foliage canopy. When in doubt, check the soil after a rain shower.

**Staggered watering.**   If some bonsai on a bench are watered every other day, it sometimes is difficult to remember which ones were watered the day before. One way to keep track is to place a small rock alongside trees that were not watered. The presence of the rock the next time around will remind you that the tree was passed the day before.

**Winter watering.**   Bonsai wintered in cold frames, garages or basements dry out quickly even without light. Concrete floors and walls absorb moisture from the air as well as water from the soil in your pots. Plants can be left dehydrated. You may have to water as often as once a week if soils are not frozen when bonsai are kept under winter protection.

**How to check drainage.**   If you water with a hose and nozzle it's almost impossible to observe whether the water drains out of the holes on the bottom of the pot. The whole pot is covered with water and obscures the water movement. To test for drainage, water with a small watering can and make sure none of the water touches the outside of the pot. Do it slowly. When the water is full to the pot rim, see how long it takes for the water to drain away and out of the holes. If the water disappears from the soil surface after a minute or two and goes right through, you are on safe ground.

But if the water just dribbles away and lingers on the soil surface, drainage is inadequate.

**Soil surface alert.**    Soil encrusted with dust and silt is impervious to water. When water cannot circulate through the soil freely, this also eliminates air which should be pulled through as water drains away. The purpose of coarse sand, fine gravel, decomposed granite or other sharp particulate substance is to provide air—not hold water. Sharp particles, therefore, encourage the growth of fibrous roots through aeration.

**Elevating containers.**    It is just as important to get rid of water once the job is done as to apply water in the first place. To help water drain away in an emergency, tilt the pot so the water drains from the side hole. If the pot contains only one hole, the container must be perfectly level. Also, it's a good idea to raise containers off display benches with small, wood sections about two inches long, one-inch wide and about a half-inch thick. Elevating the pots in this manner prevents water accumulation, encourages air circulation below the pots and helps the benches to dry.

**Leveling aids.**    Containers that are off-level will not allow water to flush uniformly through the soil. An easy way to level pots is with wood wedges. Position the wedges here and there to tilt the pots so they are true. Use a carpenter's level to find the correct position.

# 11. *Fertilizing*

There are some 16 or 17 elements plants need for proper development. Most of these elements are required in such minute quantities (trace elements), it often is difficult to determine one deficiency from another. If an established plant is lacking in one of the essentials, it does not just weaken and die; rather, it gradually becomes discolored and bedraggled looking. It appears to be stressed.

Suffice it to say, when balanced fertilizers are used regularly and in weak solutions to avoid lush growth and large foliage, most bonsai will prosper and be adequately fortified. This author uses a balanced fertilizer applied monthly during the growing season, alternating brands on the theory that each brand is just a little different from the others. There is no mystery to fertilizing and there is no need for the bonsai enthusiast to master the hard core of science and chemistry literature on the subject. A simple and established routine is all that is necessary.

**Organic vs. inorganic.** There are two types of fertilizers, organic and inorganic. *Organic* fertilizers use natural substances such as blood meal, cottonseed meal, fish emulsion, bone meal and hoof and horn meal while *inorganic* forms (soluble fertilizers) are chemically formulated. There are supporters of each class, but there also are rational reasons for their choices and use.

Organic fertilizers are slow to act, last longer in the soil, must be acted upon by soil micro-organisms to become available to the plant and they also contain some natural trace elements such as iron, zinc, magnesium, copper, etc. Chemical fertilizers, on the other hand, act fast, need no action by soil bacteria to become effective and disappear faster from the soil. They do not contain trace elements such as iron unless incorporated in the manufacturing process.

When soils constructed of fired clay aggregates are used (Turface, Terragreen, Waylite), chemical fertilizers are almost always essential because there is no soil bacteria to break down organic formulations. Weak solutions of the inorganic forms should be applied more frequently with synthetic mixes than would be the case with organic fertilizers and natural soils since organic fertilizers have a built-in "slow release" feature by their very nature. Chemical fertilizers leach out faster.

Some growers use both types of fertilizers, organic and inorganic, either by alternating the applications or under the following guidance: When air temperature is under 55°F., use inorganic; over 55°F., use organic. Since soil bacteria are not activated until air temperature is 55° or higher, organic fertilizers at lower temperature become useless. This procedure applies only when natural soil is used as the potting medium where soil bacteria are present. Whether the choice is organic or inorganic, continuous light feeding is the real secret of the fertilizing regimen.

Unless synthetic soils using the baked clay additives are innoculated with organic matter (peat moss, fir bark, compost, dehydrated cow manure) to imitate garden soil and provide the soil micro-organisms, chemical fertilizers should be used exclusively until time has had an opportunity to provide the soil bacteria that acts on organic fertilizers and makes them available for the plant to use.

During heavy rain or long periods of rain, nutritional elements can also be leached out of the soil before the plant can get to them. This is another advantage of the soluble (chemical) fertilizer forms; they become available to the roots immediately after application since they need no treatment by soil bacteria.

Finally, fertilizers are formulated for different purposes and these purposes are revealed in the percentages of the elements. High nitrogen, the first number in the sequence, produces vigorous growth, dense foliage and greater disease resistance. Such formulations usually are 25-10-10 and typical brands are Peter's, Schultz's, Miracle-Gro and Rapid-Gro. Fertilizers formulated especially for acid-loving species (azalea, some conifers) are rich in cottonseed meal. Ask for such brands as Mir-Acid and Hollytone. Some brands such as Mir-Acid and Miracle-Gro Therapy also contain trace elements in addition to the standard forms of nitrogen, phosphorus and potassium.

For low nitrogen requirements when vigorous foliage growth no longer is desired (late summer and early autumn fertilizing), use fruit, nut or tomato fertilizers.

**Soil pH control.** Until quite recently, very little had been written in contemporary publications regarding the acidity or alkalinity of potting media, nor had most bonsai growers given the matter much thought. There was general agreement that broadleaf species such as azalea and pieris required a soil on the acid side and fertilizers such as Hollytone and Mir-Acid were available for this purpose. Also, the practice of using a generous ration of peat moss in the potting soil for these species seemed to complete the academic bonsai approach to the topic.

Testing soils for pH is a relatively easy thing to do with simple color changes and test kits are available for this purpose. Agricultural extension offices also will analyze soil samples at a moderate charge and furnish recommendations for the addition of amendements to adjust the soil to the correct pH level depending on the species.

Soil reactions in container-grown plants, however, may vary from week to week and season to season depending on watering frequency, soil porosity, humidity and, indeed, "acid rain" which lately has been the target of attention by professional growers.

pH is a complicated chemical measurement to determine the relative acidity or alkalinity of the soil. The scale ranges from 1 to 14. Low numbers indicate an acid environment, high numbers indicate alkaline. Halfway in the scale, 7, is neutral.

**The meaning of pH.**  While pH is critical when considered in the light of agricultural yields and ornamental landscaping, the only importance of pH in potting soils for bonsai is its influence on the ability of the plant to absorb nutrients. And that is a very important consideration.

As indicated above, some species such as broadleaf need it on the acid side for optimum growth and vigor. Other species require a neutral soil (7.0) or slightly above which is on the alkaline side. Nothing will grow in the extremes at either end.

It is difficult to understand just why a plant can't utilize the three main fertilizer elements—nitrogen (N), phosphorus (P) and potassium (K)—unless the soil is the correct pH for the species, but it is a fact steeped in science and chemistry.

Other than using a test kit with color indicators or the pH testing instrument, how do we determine if the pH value of the potting medium is correct for the plant species? Mostly by referring to the species' natural environment and then duplicating the pH value in the pot—or by observing a plant's reaction based on discoloring of the foliage—and by trial and error observations of experienced growers at nurseries, extension offices or aboreta. If foliage yellows, however, in spite of a regular fertilizing regimen, it is a good indication that the pH is off. In many species, it makes no difference whether the pH is slightly below neutral or slightly above.

**Plant pH requirements.**  Just which species require which pH has never been clearly defined in the bonsai literature and differences of opinion abound. The following guidelines, however, have been established by professional growers: Known acidloving species (5.5 to 6.5 pH) are birch, azalea, camellia, gardenia and the majority of dwarf conifers. Species that prefer higher soil pH are Chinese juniper, Scots pine, Eastern white pine (Strobus), apples, taxus and cedrus and cypress (Hinoki) species. Deciduous species appear to have a wide tolerance of pH variations. Western species of bonsai all require a higher pH. Even if you do not know whether the species to be tested belongs in an acid, alkaline or neutral medium, you can suspect that something may be wrong if the plant fails to respond to fertilizer. Incorrect pH locks in the nutrients and fertilizer applications are wasted. By checking the soil pH you may get a clue. If the pH is too high or too low, this may be the answer. If the pH appears normal, something else may be wrong. The important thing is to look for the extreme in pH.

**Applying ashes.**  A common practice is to apply hardwood ashes to the soils of yellowing junipers. Since hardwood ashes are slightly alkaline through the high calcium content (up to 45%), this raises the soil pH enough to produce a beneficial influence on the juniper's ability to nourish itself, as determined by the color of the foliage. The wood ashes, therefore, are equivalent to adding lime to the soil although wood ashes also contain 5% potash, one of the elements in a balanced fertilizer. Do not neglect other fertilizers when wood ashes are used to adjust soil pH. Wood ashes do not provide nitrogen and only small amounts of phosphorus and potassium.

It merits mention here that another cause of yellowing junipers is infestation by spider mite which may be mistaken for incorrect soil pH. Always be certain you are treating for the correct symptom.

Professional nurserymen are well aware of the importance of soil pH and they use soil acidifiers and soil alkalizers in wholesale proportions. The nurserymen want to reduce stress and deal with the problems in growth that affect their bottom lines; we want to avoid stress for the sake of beautiful bonsai.

It stands to reason that bonsai originating in areas that require a soil of a particular pH should be potted with a soil of the same value. Your author has followed the practice of "liming" species brought in from the Western states including a Ponderosa pine, several Western junipers and a Texas elm (U. Crassafolia). All these species, transplanted from their natural environments, have flourished in containers. A teaspoonful of dolomitic lime is spread over the soil surface once a month during the growing season.

**The end result.**  From these observations, it is obvious that soil pH alters the solubility of soil nutrients and, therefore, the fertilizer's efficiency. If the soil environment as to pH is not correct for the species, the fertilizer becomes ineffective due to the plant's inability to absorb nutrition. Some plants are able to survive a wide pH spectrum while others can tolerate only a very specific range. Most species used for bonsai grow best in neutral or slightly acidic soils of pH 6.5 to 7.0.

It also appears as if there is no critical or fixed survival point at moderately high or low pH differences for specific species but, rather, there appears to be considerable latitude. Acid loving species will tolerate a pH just above the acid side and, likewise, alkaline oriented material will endure a pH environment just below the alkaline level.

As bonsai are watered, soils tend to revert to the ambient pH of the soil composition. Peat moss, added to the original potting medium to lower pH, decomposes and its acid value disappears. Likewise, when lime is added to the soil to raise the pH, this also leaches away through repeated waterings.

When an acid-type fertilizer is used regularly for known acid-loving species, the acidity level is restored at each feeding. And the monthly application of a teaspoonful of granular dolomitic lime spread over the soil surface should also correct the pH for alkaline oriented species.

Extremes in either direction can prove harmful, but the criterion in pH requirements is plant appearance. If we avoid stress by improving a plant's ability to absorb nutrients, the response will be apparent in vigorous and attractive growth.

**When to fertilize.**    Apply the first application in April after buds appear and growth begins. Do not fertilize in spring if bonsai are to be repotted at that time. Wait one month after potting and only if new growth is apparent. From May through September, fertilize once each month using half-strength solutions. Fertilize twice a month if quarter-strength solutions are used. Do not fertilize after the middle of August with high nitrogen as it will encourage the development of tender growth which may not be winter hardy.

**Fertilizer concentrations.**    Frequent, weak applications of fertilizers are better than occasional stronger doses. A weak application would be quarter-strength or less; strong applications are half-strength or more.

Plant deficiencies are very difficult to determine except through elaborate laboratory analyses and, even then, it is doubtful whether the findings prevail from week to week for potted material such as bonsai. There are too many variables that alter nutrition levels such as watering frequency, light, drainage and organic matter present in the soil. You must rely on your sense of observation to determine deficiencies. If leaves or needles are lighter or darker than normal—or if leaf veins are more pronounced (an indication of iron deficiency)—or

if the edges or needle tips begin to yellow or brown without insect or weather damage—you should suspect a nutritional need.

If you apply fertilizer on the basis of recommendations from commercial growers and experts who develop plant material for shows and awards, you will be misled. These afficionados use fertilizers to enhance growth. In bonsai, we use fertilizers only to sustain growth. We do not want rampant growth and large leaves for commercial use or competitive attraction. We want good color and growth maintenance, so we fertilize discreetly—weak solutions and often—just enough to keep the plant in trim.

**Rainfall and fertilizer.**    Following periods of heavy rain, it is a good idea to apply a dose of fertilizer. Nutrients in the soil may become leached away faster than would be the case with a normal watering schedule.

**Fertilizer and wintering.**    Plant material newly purchased from a nursery may contain sustained-release fertilizer scattered on the soil surface. This method of fertilizing is in wide use and quite effective since nutrients are released with each watering.

This type of fertilizer usually lasts about six months before it is entirely spent, although there are some formulations that release nutrients for shorter intervals. The only problem with these fertilizers is that bonsai moved to winter quarters may have new growth stimulated before the new growth has had a chance to harden off, only to die back when hit by frost.

Plants that contain sustained-release fertilizer—and it is apparent when you observe tiny colored balls on the soil surface—should not be allowed to freeze. Winter them in a cold garage or other unheated protected atmosphere.

**Nutrition alternate.**    Many bonsai growers change fertilizer brands alternately, even with the same nutrition proportions, in the belief that trace elements may be available in one brand that may be lacking in another. One good interlude in the fertilizer regimen is to use Superthrive instead of a regular formulation. This fortified brand combines vitamins and hormones that are known to be beneficial to plant growth and which may be lacking in standard formulations. Superthrive also is a favorite among many growers as a quick "fix" for new plantings. It is sprayed on the roots before potting and a solution (10 drops to a gallon of water) is applied for the first watering.

**An early feeder.**    Korean and Kingsville box varieties put out one surge of new growth in early spring. In order to make fertilizer available when most needed, and to encourage additional new growth surges, spread a teaspoonful (for small pots) or a tablespoonful (for large pots) of cottonseed meal over the soil surface in

February. Since cottonseed meal is an organic fertilizer and slow-acting, it will be available when the plants need it most.

**Acidifying soils.**    Azalea and other broadleaf species require soil on the acid pH range. This adjustment can be made with peat moss, which is on the acid side, by adding more of it to the soil mix. You could also use an acidifier fertilizer such as Hollytone, which is made with cottonseed meal, or Mir-Acid which uses chemical acidifier agents. Another suggestion is to mix two tablespoons of vinegar to a quart of water and drench the soil. This should serve only as an emergency measure for altering the soil pH quickly. The acidifier fertilizers will take care of the long range pH consideration.

**Last meal.**    Give bonsai a final dose of fertilizer before dormancy sets in to create a reservoir of nutrition when the plant resumes growth. There is no risk of stimulating new growth that may die back due to freezing temperatures. Once dormancy has been established due to temperature and light reduction, the plant will remain dormant until growth-stimulating light and temperature are resumed. The rewards of good nutrition become apparent after new growth resumes in the spring.

**Fertilizing basic.**    The object in a fertilizing regimen is to keep bonsai healthy, not encourage an abundance of new growth which may spoil a styling. If too much new growth is observed when you dilute fertilizers 50%, reduce the dilution to 25%. For example, a 20-20-20 fertilizer diluted by half becomes 10-10-10 which is still a strong application. The best criterion is foliage appearance. If you observe rank growth and long internodes, reduce the feeding.

**Fertilizing and potting soils.**    One advantage in using screened loam in the potting medium is the presence of organic matter in the soil which provides a modicum of nutrition while the plant is getting started. If the loam is sterilized, however, soil bacteria also disappear and the nutrition caused by the action of these organisms on organic matter goes with it.

Also, with synthetic soil additives such as Perlite, Vermiculite, Terragreen and Turface, nutrients in the potting medium are completely lacking. Peat moss contains just a trace, if any. If you use these additives, or if you sterilize natural soil, more frequent fertilizing is necessary, not larger doses. In this way, you compensate for the nutrition deficiency in the potting mix.

Of course, fertilizer should never be used regardless of the potting medium until the plant shows visual signs of growth. When new growth is apparent, start applying weak fertilizer solutions, about a quarter strength. Frequent, weak solutions of fertilizer are always better than stronger applications applied less frequently.

**Hold the nitrogen.**    Eliminate nitrogen fertilizing in late autumn. Nitrogen may stimulate soft, late growth which can be nipped by early frost before it gets a chance to harden for winter protection. Use a fertilizer formulation without the "N" factor or a low "N" factor. These formulations are not readily available at garden centers because the market for them is rather limited. You can formulate one yourself with phosphorus and potassium only by using equal parts of bonemeal and superphosphate.

**Feather rock hint.**    To encourage a mossy, aged look in the rock's appearance, soak the rock (before applying plants) in a tub of water to which has been added one-half teaspoon of fish emulsion per gallon of water. Also, the roots of plants secured to porous rocks such as feather rock, volcanic rock and tufa rock penetrate the material to a remarkable degree in search of moisture. When fertilizing the soil or muck of these plantings, also apply fertilizer solution to the entire rock to provide a reservoir of nutrition within the interspaces.

**Yellowing foliage.**    In addition to infestation with spider mites, lack of nitrogen and incorrect soil pH, discolored foliage frequently is the result of iron deficiency. Deciduous species suffering from chlorosis (iron deficiency) are easily recognized. Leaves become mottled with yellow areas while veins become a darker green. On evergreens, the needles or foliage (azalea, taxus, cypress) may turn completely yellow. An annual dose of chelated iron will supply the plant's needs for a full growing season. A product produced by the makers of Miracle-Gro is Miracle-Gro Therapy, a balanced fertilizer, plus iron, zinc, copper and manganese to supply the trace elements. Remember, in order for these trace elements to become available to the plant, the soil pH must also be correct for the species.

**Fertilizer choices.**    For a quick fix early in the growing season, in a medium using natural soil, water-soluble chemical fertilizers will get the plant off to a good start. As the season progresses, organic fertilizers—which are slower to act—will supply adequate nutrition without the root-burn hazard of chemical formulations.

A good home-made formulation of organic materials is the "Three Meals" method, one-third each of blood meal, bone meal and cottonseed meal. The latter two ingredients are slow-acting and not completely soluble. Blood meal, on the other hand, is soluble and fast-acting and a natural organic nitrogen source. Use monthly June through September for developing bonsai at the rate of one-half teaspoonful for a six inch pot and larger pots in proportion. For mature bonsai, use only twice during the growing season. Spread the "Three Meals" on the soil surface previously moistened and scratch it in. Nutrition is released with each watering. This is more easily controlled than the slow-release fertilizers which have become popular. In the latter, if an excess amount is applied, it stays.

**Note nitrogen sources.**  Package labels for fertilizers must, by law, reveal information that indicates sources of the various elements. It is especially important to note the sources of nitrogen when applying fertilizer to synthetic soils. Since these fired clay materials lack bacteria that break down organic fertilizers, chemical fertilizers should always be used. Nitrogen availability, however, varies in these formulations according to the nitrogen sources.

Avoid fertilizers that use ammonium sulfate, urea or di-ammonium phosphate as the main sources of nitrogen. Look for those that contain *calcium* or *sodium* nitrate. Just as soil bacteria are necessary to break down the organic fertilizers, soil organisms are also necessary to break down the ammonia compounds. Since these organisms are absent in synthetic soils, the result is your plant receives a lower nitrogen level than the package label implies. Nitrogen availability to the plant is the important consideration, but synthetic soil mixes are not taken into account when availability is calculated. It makes no difference about nitrogen sources when natural soil is used for potting, although organic fertilizers also work faster when fortified with *nitrate* nitrogen (calcium or sodium nitrate).

**Slow-release fertilizers.**  Manufactured slow-release fertilizers utilize a polymer resin coating over the chemical pellets to retard and time the solubility of the active ingredients. They are inorganic and, once applied, they can last all season. The Japanese version of slow-release fertilizers are known as fertilizer balls or "dumplings" made from the fermentation residue of the rape seed after the oil is removed. The U.S. equivalent of rape seed is cottonseed or flaxseed (linseed). The source is organic. A homemade version can be formulated by combining cottonseed meal, blood meal and bone meal, adding water and spreading the slurry on a shallow tray to dry and harden after which the mass is cut into one-inch squares for application on soil surfaces.

The catalyst of all the slow-release fertilizers is water. In a heavy and prolonged rain, over-fertilizing can result. While convenient, you also have lost control with the time-release formulas over the amount of fertilizer you want your plants to have.

**Fertilizing rock plantings.**  An application of the "Three Meals" (blood meal, bone meal and cottonseed meal) spread over various portions of the rock or slab planting will release nutrients at each watering. Apply a quarter teaspoonful to each plant once weekly during the growing season for three weeks. This procedure,

however, often results in "caking" at the soil surface and discoloring of moss.

Liquid fertilizers applied with a spout to rock plantings cannot penetrate the same as plantings in conventional containers. More often than not, the dry surface of the moss and muck potting medium repels the liquid and it runs off uselessly. To prevent this, first spray lightly with plain water to break the surface tension. Then apply the fertilizer solution which will soak quickly into the soil.

**Vague fertilizer instructions.**  Label instructions for some fertilizers provide two sets of application rates. They detail concentrations for (a), potted house plants and, (b), outdoor species such as pines, junipers, etc. Which instructions apply for bonsai which are *both* potted plants and outdoor material? The dilemma is compounded when you consider that the difference in application rates is quite substantial.

For example, one of the popular brand 20-20-20 fertilizers recommends varying amounts of material for potted indoor plants ranging from ¼ tsp. per gallon of water to a full tsp. per gallon depending on light conditions. For evergreen, deciduous species and shrubs grown outdoors, the recommendation is 1-½ *tablespoons* per gallon of water. Which would you use for an evergreen species *potted* plant which combines both the above specifications? The author's recommendation is to follow the instructions for houseplants, half strength. Reason: Fertilizers applied to plants growing in the ground are dispersed over a wide area; fertilizers in bonsai pots are in more prolonged contact. A small amount in a bonsai pot goes a long way.

**Using proportional sprayers for fertilizers.**
Growers with extensive bonsai collections will find proportional sprayers a convenient means for fertilizer application. These sprayers, which have become popular for spraying insecticides, can be pre-set for desired dilutions. There is an added advantage in using a spray for fertilizers rather than a watering can in that foliage absorption can produce faster nutritional results. Of course, the soil should also be purged with a sprayer the same as you would do with a watering can.

To use a proportional sprayer, if the manufacturer's instructions call for a teaspoonful of liquid concentrate to a gallon of water, simply pour a small quantity of fertilizer in the sprayer container. Set the dial for an output of one teaspoonful per gallon of water. The spray solution will come out of the sprayer with the correct dilution.

When a powder concentrate is used rather than a liquid, pre-mixing of powder with a small quantity of water is required. If instructions call for a tablespoon of powder concentrate to a gallon of water, dissolve a tablespoon of powder into five ounces of water which is equivalent to ten tablespoons. When the dial is set at "10 tablespoons," the sprayer will siphon off the entire five ounces of mix at the correct dosage of one tablespoon of powder to a gallon of water.

If you want one teaspoon of powder to a gallon of water, make a pre-mix of one teaspoonful of powder concentrate into five ounces of water for a gallon of finished spray. Again, set the dial at "10 tablespoons." The solution will be siphoned off at the correct mix of one teaspoon per gallon of water.

Each of the foregoing examples provides spray for a gallon of mix. For multiple gallons of finished spray, multiply the proportions by whatever quantity of finished spray you desire up to the capacity of the sprayer container. Just remember, each five ounces of pre-mixed solution represents a gallon of diluted spray at the desired proportion when the dial is set for 10 tablespoons (two tablespoons equal one ounce).

Any undissolved particles of powder may clog the sprayer openings. For certain wettable powders where the rate per gallon of dilution is too high to mix freely with water, or with highly viscous liquids, mix at the half rate and make two applications. Also, some powders may not dissolve freely due to fillers. If you observe a sediment after you pre-mix the powder with water, screen the pre-mix through a paint filter (40 mesh screen).

**Fertilizing summary.** (1) Use organic fertilizers when loam is used in the potting mix. Organic fertilizers need soil bacteria to decompose organic substances (cottonseed meal, compost, fish emulsion, etc.). (2) Use soluble fertilizers (chemical source) when synthetic amendments are used as the main potting medium. These soils contain little or no micro-organisms which are necessary to activate fertilizers. Soluble fertilizers need no catalyst and act faster, but they also leach away faster. So chemical fertilizers should be applied more frequently. (3) Organic fertilizers are not activated by soil bacteria when air temperature is below 50°F. Use inorganic fertilizers at this temperature or lower. (4) Soil pH is important to bonsai because it adjusts the plant's ability to assimilate and metabolize nutrients. If a plant fails to respond to a regular fertilizer regimen by showing good color and growth, the soil pH may be incorrect. This is especially important in acid-loving plants (azalea) and the opposite, alkaline-oriented species, such as juniper. Species grown in our Western states also require higher pH soils.

# 12. *Winter Protection*

Protecting bonsai from the ravages of nature is no problem for those living in areas of the country where temperatures seldom go below 30°F., where snowfall is sparse or non-existent or where climatic conditions are moderated by the nation's geography. Temperature extremes in large sections of the country, however, play havoc with tender bonsai if they are not given protection even when they are kept in correct temperature zones for the species.

A "Weather Watch" for winter protection should start when temperature stays consistently at 40°F. or below. Nighttime temperature during October and November often drops into the low thirties or twenties for short periods of time, but it is the consistent low below 40° when plans for protection should be made.

In some northern areas, this could occur as early as the end of September. In other sections, bonsai need not be placed under protection until the first week of December. And in sections south of Washington, DC, only moderate protection may be necessary. Tropical or semi-tropical plant species maintained in cold areas must be placed in a greenhouse or kept indoors before the onset of temperature in the 40's outdoors.

Placing bonsai under winter protection too soon is not recommended. Hardy species must be conditioned for dormancy. They should be allowed to get "nipped" by frost several times before transfer to winter quarters.

Hardiness characteristics of all growing things are geared by genetics. Killing points are increased as temperatures fall from 30°F. As day length gets shorter, growth stops and helps to increase hardiness. Trees also prepare for dormancy by hardening and other protective measures around growing tips. Material purchased locally usually is safe, whereas plants transferred from a correct hardiness zone to a zone of less hardiness may get into trouble. Bonsai lacking such hardiness are the most vulnerable and it is not uncommon to bring such material in from out-of-doors to winter in a heated greenhouse or treated as indoor bonsai for ultimate protection until it is safe to restore the plants outdoors again.

Severe winter weather seems not to affect some species of dubious hardiness such as the various buxus and azalea varieties where discoloring of the foliage appears to be the only consequence of *protected* winter exposure

outdoors. In sub-tropical areas where there is a risk of sudden freezing temperatures, bonsai must also be protected the same as in colder areas. Some sub-tropical species such as buttonwood and bald cypress may languish when exposed to frost.

**Environmental changes.** Winter hardiness in the zone of current occupation is, by far, the critical factor. Many coniferous bonsai, especially the Western junipers, just will not tolerate the severe and continuous temperatures encountered in the Midwest and East without adequate protection, despite the fact that they are also exposed to severe weather in their native environments. The difference lies in the variation of *ground* temperatures between these sections of the country.

Hardiness zones are determined on the basis of average minimum temperatures. The lower the number, the more severe the temperature range. These temperatures, however, represent *air* temperatures, not temperatures in the root zone. For plants grown in containers, therefore, there are two distinct areas of winter hardiness—*top* hardiness and *root* hardiness. There can be a difference in these two areas by as much as 20°. The important contrast is this: While the foliage, stems and branches can live safely in contact with bitter cold in a correct hardiness zone, the *roots* in a bonsai pot exposed to *air* temperatures in these zones may suffer. Stress caused by severe cold may be fatal. If air and root zone temperature could be kept at the same, there would be no problem.

Unfortunately, there is no hardiness zone data available for roots similar to that established for top growth. It is a factor that must be reckoned with only in bonsai because, here, both roots and top are exposed to the same ambient temperature ranges in contrast to trees growing in nature. Nature has no need to "insulate" roots from the low air temperatures encountered in bonsai pots. Deep-down natural soil is the insulator.

Also, roots in the ground do not "harden off" as do the tops in preparation for winter exposure. Roots maintained in the same temperature as the air, even for potted species in correct temperature zones for foliage, may perish long before any top damage is apparent. We must recognize these facts when we expose our bonsai in pots to winter air temperatures.

These admonitions are not intended to suggest that the hope of wintering bonsai away from native temperature zones is remote. Not at all. Many individuals in the New York area successfully winter such tropical and semi-tropical species as bald cypress, ficus and buttonwood which are native to Florida and many specimens of the coveted California juniper are thriving by wintering in cold basements and sheltered cold pits. The big factor is simple protection.

**Winter protection objectives.**    The main objective is to maintain dormancy until weather permits full exposure to the outdoors again. It's not the cold, but the freeze/thaw sequence we should avoid. Freeze/thaw happens in nature all the time and this is known among nurserymen as "winter kill." Protection against sun and wind checks winter kill. Here are protection guidelines:

1. Plant bonsai, pots and all, in the ground, preferably in a location to the east of a building, house or protective planting such as a line of shrubs. Placing them where they will be exposed to prevailing northwest winter winds or sun will increase the risk. Mulch the plants with leaves, a mound of soil, wood chips, salt hay, pine needles and even pine branches.

In addition, surround the bonsai with a burlap wind break. The important consideration is to protect the bonsai from wind and sun. Burlap is better than polyethylene because it is low in cost, screens out the sun and is easy to set up. You can also used discarded drapery, old sheets and other material that can be stapled to stakes in the ground. Stakes should be pounded into the ground about eight inches deep. Be sure to get them in before the ground freezes hard, otherwise you will have to wait for a temporary thaw. The first week of December is about right in freezing areas.

2. Apply anti-desiccant spray to keep foliage from drying out. This is especially effective for evergreen and broadleaf species. This harmless spray, Wilt-Pruf or other brands, coats the needles with a transparent covering that allows light to penetrate, but insulates foliage against dehydration. In winter, on a warm day, top growth loses moisture which roots cannot replace because the soil is frozen. When you take steps to help foliage retain moisture, the chance of winter damage is reduced.

Wilt-Pruf must be applied when the temperature is above 40°. Two sprayings are sufficient for protection until spring. When spraying, keep the can about 18 inches away from the plant. Propellants in the aerosol can come out at an extremely low temperature and this can be damaging, too. A water-miscible form of Wilt-Pruf also is available for home mixing with water, but it is a nuisance to apply with a pressure sprayer. Aerosol application is the most convenient although higher in cost for extensive application.

3. Store bonsai in a protected area such as the ov-erhang of a house, under a crawl space or the storage area under a swimming pool.

4. A cold basement area can be ventilated for temperature control, or an unheated garage or shed, are ideal solutions for winter protection. The aim is (a) to keep plants dormant until ready to be brought outdoors, (b) to avoid light that may encourage growth during mild days and, (c) to protect the plants from wind that may dehydrate the tops. In these environments, the roots are well taken care of.

**Light and dormancy.**    The question often is raised as to whether bonsai require light while maintained under winter protection. The all-important factor in making this determination is the temperature range in the area where the bonsai are stored for the winter.

Deciduous and coniferous species require a cold period of six to eight weeks in order to break dormancy and grow again. Deciduous bonsai, defoliated and dormant, require no light and can be kept in relative darkness or dim light until dormancy ends which becomes evident through swelling buds.

It's a little different with conifers—pine, spruce, juniper, etc. When these species are wintered in environments that remain below freezing, dormancy is complete and light is unnecessary—if the temperature stays below freezing. Where full dormancy is not complete, however, and temperatures fluctuate above and below 45°F. which is the dormancy maximum, new growth may be encouraged and some light will be needed. In this situation, bonsai are in a state of suspended animation—not fully dormant, nor in a state of active growth. Some respiration, no matter how slight, does occur.

For growers in areas where winters are not severe and where dormancy for evergreen species is never complete, light is essential. In the very cold regions like the middle west and New England sections of the country, it is common practice to winter bonsai in darkened cold frames and sheds. Light in these environments is unnecessary.

*Strong* light during dormancy is unwise for both deciduous and coniferous species. Growth may be stimulated only to die back should plants be subjected to a sudden temperature drop. Spring is the most dangerous time of the year with respect to dormancy. New growth becomes evident due to mild weather, but strong wind and sun can quickly decimate this new growth. Protection against wind and sun becomes more important in the spring than, perhaps, at any other time during the dormant period.

Winter protection is just that. It does not mean coddling your bonsai. Hardy specimens need the cold. Once the soil in pots becomes frozen under protection, they should stay frozen until it's time for dormancy to end. When that time comes, the air temperature will thaw the pots—and then you will know.

## WINTER PROTECTION MEASURES

*Some bonsai can be set on*
*bricks beneath a clump of trees....*

*... and protected with burlap*
*stapled to the tree trunks.*

## WINTER PROTECTION MEASURES

Bonsai of borderline hardiness can be protected under the overhang of a house where the temperature remains about the same as out in the open, but no wind or sun....

... then the perimeter of the overhang is enclosed with burlap stapled to the house. The plants should be watered when the ground is not frozen.

Finally, the bonsai most vulnerable to winter damage can be lined up on benches in an unheated garage. An emergency source of heat can be provided with a soil heater zigzagged below the pots, plugged in for supplemental heat, if necessary. The pots should be placed on strips of wood to avoid direct contact with the heater cable. Ambient temperature in unheated garages is approximately 10° F. higher than outside temperature. Weekly watering is necessary.

**Dormancy data.** Trees in nature stay dormant until they acquire a specific number of hours, depending on the species, below 45°F. This is called a "chilling requirement" and it is genetically controlled for each variety. Apricot, quince and fig are better adapted to warmer climates because they require less than 1,000 hours of accumulated cold. Apples, crabapples, cherry and plum require about 50 cumulative days under 45° to break dormancy which is about 1,200 hours of cold exposure.

Bonsai that receive inadequate chilling to satisfy their genetic requirements to break dormancy will not do well the following season and they will continue to decline. This applies to both deciduous and coniferous species. Signs of insufficient chilling are delays in leafing and blooming or a scattered bloom over a long period of time. Blossoms may drop off. If flower buds have been pruned away during the process of training, however, blossoms will also fail to appear.

While roots have a lower tolerance for cold than the tops, the opposite is true when it comes to the *growth* of roots. Roots will continue to grow at lower temperatures (40°F.) than the tops (about 50°F.). Roots function best at soil temperatures of 65° to 80°F. Above 104°F. root tips are killed. This can be a significant problem for bonsai exposed to full sun, all day, in dark colored pots.

**Dormancy variables.** Bonsai kept under protection for the winter (garages, cold frames, cool basements) emerge from dormancy about two weeks before their counterparts in nature. Maples winterized often are in full leaf when those in the ground are in the swollen bud stage. Apples, if brought out too soon, frequently revert to dormancy and repeat the dormant cycle, often misleading the grower to conclude that the specimen expired. Wait a while before you come to that conclusion.

Azalea sometimes suffer winter injury and some branches may look dead. Avoid pruning these apparent casualties. It may require a month of culture outdoors before turgidity is re-established. Chances are, new growth will sprout as late as mid-summer and, oftentimes, even the next year. Azalea sprouts easily from adventitious buds in old wood. For wintering, allow azalea to get "nipped" with frost before placing them under cover for the winter which means sheltered from wind and sun or an unheated garage where temperature does not fall much below 30°F.

**The meaning of winter-kill.** Low temperature slows down the transfer of moisture from roots to top. When accompanied by high wind and sun, desiccation occurs at a faster rate than the tissues can replace. Whereas bonsai may survive severe exposure during deep dormancy and in shade where moisture demand is at low ebb, early new growth stimulated by mild weather can be ruinous. This happens in nature all the time. When a branch dies back due to dehydration, the tree grows another branch somewhere else to compensate for the loss. For esthetic reasons, we cannot afford to be so casual about branch replacement in bonsai. The new branch may not be precisely where you want it.

**Winter styling observations.** Deciduous species are especially revealing during dormancy. When plants are inspected at this time, notice whether the branches on top have developed more than those below. This suggests that the lower branches may have been shaded from sunlight. When upper branches are allowed to grow too long, they screen out sunlight from others. While you are inspecting your bonsai during winter, look for crossing branches, too. They are quite apparent when bonsai are defoliated. You may have scrupulously removed crossing branches when the bonsai were styled, but these maverick branches have a habit of cropping up from time to time unnoticed. Also remove branches growing inward. They will die anyway.

**Winter watering.** When pots are wintered outdoors on top of the ground or planted in the ground below the pot rims, mulched and protected from sun and wind with burlap screens, winter snows and rain will provide adequate moisture. The "frozen assets" also will supply moisture during thaws. Remember, when bonsai are fully dormant and screened from winter sun and wind, very little moisture is needed, anyway.

In winter, bonsai need protection from *dehydration* due to extreme cold, wind and sun. This becomes a problem, however, when plants are wintered under shelters such as cold frames, house overhangs and garages where no natural moisture is available. In such situations, soils should never be allowed to become bone dry. On mild days, when the soil is not frozen, water lightly.

Winter-hardy species growing in correct temperature zones can stand cold to the maximum ranges indicated in hardiness-zone maps for foliage. Problems arise when temperatures moderate and moisture is lacking in the soil to supply the needs above.

When bonsai are placed under winter protection at the start of the season (November and the early part of December), water thoroughly and continue to water as long as the soil is not frozen. Then, if a prolonged freeze comes along, do not water. By keeping the soil moist at all times, even after this moisture freezes hard, the plant is prepared when there is a demand for moisture after a thaw.

It may sound like a contradiction, but dry soil around the roots of a plant is *colder* than soil that is adequately moisturized. Water has a buffering action that keeps soil temperature around the root zone favorable for the plants. Before it can freeze solid, water gives off a tremendous amount of heat relative to its surroundings.

This heat by-product of freezing serves to keep the soil around the roots above the root-killing temperature which, for some plants, is about 20°F.

The resultant soil-moisture medium could be considered as "slush," a mixture of water and ice crystals. Winter damage from roots destroyed through excessive cold can thus be avoided by the mere presence of adequate soil moisture. The more water the soil contains, the longer the temperature in the vicinity of the roots will be prevented from dropping below the freezing mark. Roots can't rot because soil bacteria are dormant.

Once snow arrives, the deeper it is the better for the plants. Snow is nature's best blanket. In addition to supplying constant moisture, which is converted to soil heat as it melts and starts to freeze, snow keeps plants protected from harsh winds and winter sun. As long as snow remains on the plants, no harm is done. Damage comes when snow is too heavy and breaks off branches, or when it is a mixture of ice and snow. At these times, it should be gently brushed away.

If bonsai are wintered in garages, sheds or cold frames, pots should be checked frequently for moisture. Do not water if the soil is frozen. The soil in bonsai pots which are wintered in garages dries out more rapidly than bonsai sheltered in cold frames or other outdoor environments. The porosity of concrete floors and cement block walls attracts moisture. This is especially evident as the sun gets warmer and ambient temperatures in garages tend to rise. Check pots for dryness at least weekly.

To improve humidity levels, garage floors should be sprayed occasionally with a hose. When garage windows cloud up due to condensation, humidity is more than adequate.

**Beware car exhaust.** Exhaust from cars can be toxic if not allowed to dissipate. Just how and why exhaust fumes can be hazardous to plants, especially those in dormancy, has never been fully explained. Nevertheless, if a car is pulled out of the garage immediately after starting and allowed to warm up outdoors—if the garage door is kept open ten or fifteen minutes when the car is brought in and taken out—these precautions are sufficient. The author has used an unheated garage to winter approximately thirty bonsai for more than twenty years and has never suffered a loss, with temperature dropping to a low of 20°F. for brief periods. A soil heater is laid over the benches and plugged in for supplemental heat in case of an emergency.

**Wintering nursery material.** Newly purchased nursery material in cans or burlap should be placed in the ground and mulched with salt hay or leaves rather than stored in the open. Due to the heavy fertilizing regimens of commercial growers, nursery grown material will have masses of new, tender fibrous roots which need extra winter protection. An unheated garage or

shed also would be ideal. Never allow balled or canned material recently purchased from a nursery to winter unprotected.

**Winter pruning and wiring.** January and February are the best times to start training deciduous species such as apple, elm and maple when branch configuration is apparent. Foliage may have obscured long shoots during the growing season as well as crossing branches and unwanted growth that may have upset the overall shape of the tree. The branches of deciduous species are more supple during dormancy and before sap starts to flow, so wiring is easier. Take advantage of the winter months to observe deciduous species when they are defoliated and before the spring potting season starts with a vengeance. Conifers kept above 32° during the winter months and tropical and semi-tropical species stored indoors or in a greenhouse can also be pruned and wired during winter.

An important caution: Pruning during winter must be done outdoors or in the area where the bonsai is still under protection and dormant such as a garage. New growth may be stimulated on any material brought indoors even for a short period of time. When replaced outdoors, this new growth may be winter-killed due to the sudden temperature change. The other option is to keep the newly-pruned bonsai indoors until frost-risk in your area has passed.

**Horticultural spring.** The first sign of spring in the horticultural world is not March 21st, but December 21st. On the latter date, the sun climbs higher in the sky and the days start to get longer by a few seconds each day. Consider yourself lucky if bonsai wintered outdoors are covered with a layer of snow which has been called "poor man's mulch." Winter sun and wind are more deadly than cold.

**First wintering.** Newly-potted bonsai must not be exposed to severe winter weather. Root pruning stimulates new growth quickly and the new root system may not be ready to tackle winter temperature extremes. Evergreens, which lose moisture through the foliage in winter, are likely to be the first victims to premature exposure. Keep newly potted bonsai under greater protection the first winter. An ideal environment would be an unheated garage or cold greenhouse.

**Few bonsai to winter.** If you have only a handful of bonsai to care for during the winter, put them in a basement window well on the sheltered side of the house. If drainage might be a problem, set the pots over bricks. Cover everything with mulch up to the lower branches.

In situations where you bury bonsai in the ground, and this also is a good solution when you have just a few bonsai to winter, remove the pot if it is important to you rather than risk breakage in the ground. Make a temporary container with aluminum foil around the root ball for easy lifting from the ground in spring and replacement in the pot.

There are as many variations for wintering bonsai as there are bonsai growers. The basic theme is: mulch the bottom, shade the top.

**Selecting nursery material.** Winter or late autumn is the best time to shop the nurseries. The leaves are off deciduous stock and the tree stands naked, revealing all its beauty and flaws.

**Drastic surgery.** A good time to amputate heavy branches or create extensive driftwood is during the winter months when bonsai is frozen solid in the container or ground. The material is held rigid as if gripped by a vice and there is no movement during the operation to disturb the soil and dislodge the tree.

**The cold treatment.** It's better to keep bonsai outdoors until they get "nipped" a few times by light frost of about 30°F. before they are placed under winter protection. It hastens dormancy and prepares the bonsai for a winter rest. This, of course, does not apply to tender tropicals. Hardy conifers and evergreens will benefit from a preliminary exposure to cold.

**Plants vs. humans.** People tend to treat plants as they do themselves. They "bandage" a pruning wound with a dressing to seal it against disease organisms and to promote healing. According to current thinking, this is more a cosmetic gesture than a scientific necessity.

Some people spread mulch to keep the soil "warm." Nothing will make soil any "warmer" than the temperature around it, except when heat is applied through an external source such as a soil heater or a heater fan. The purpose of a mulch is to keep the soil frozen and insulate the plant from alternate thawing and freezing. That is why a mulch should be applied to bonsai in the ground *after* the first hard frost.

**Wintering preparations.** Certain measures to prepare the bonsai for wintering are good insurance and avoid stress when spring awakens the plants. The esthetic preparations involve removal of wire to avoid scars, even if the branch has to be re-wired in the spring. Horticultural preparations include removal of moss from the soil surface to allow air and water to penetrate freely when the bonsai are brought outdoors again. It is especially important to eliminate liverwort growths, the star-shaped ground cover that will grow rampant unless checked. Pick it out with a tweezer and scrape the soil clean of any remaining rudimentary growth. At the same time, lightly cultivate the soil surface to break up any caking that may have formed from fertilizer.

**Wintering indoor bonsai.** Indoor bonsai kept outdoors for the summer should be placed in shade for at least a month prior to moving them indoors for the winter. This allows them to become acclimated to reduced light. They should be brought in well before temperatures drop. Also, bonsai in small containers need extra care from the elements in winter, even if the species is grown in the correct temperature zone. Small pots and soil volume make small bonsai especially vulnerable.

**Ides of March.** Spring, with variable temperatures from below freezing to relative warmth, is the most dangerous time of the year for all growing things. March winds and sun can seriously injure tender, new growth.

**Terminating winter protection.** Don't be too hasty to bring them out. Tender roots and foliage may be injured by a late spring frost. The object of wintering bonsai is to maintain dormancy until the risk of freezing weather ends. Maintain a freeze watch until a week or so beyond the date of last frost in your area. Expose them gradually to full light for at least a week. Dappled sun or shaded sunlight is satisfactory. Natural plants growing in the ground can cope with the vagaries of spring weather, but bonsai coddled indoors for a season may not be able to make a smooth transition if exposed to outdoor conditions too quickly.

**Frost hazard.** Sometimes we mis-calculate and frost can form on new growth before we realize it. The real danger arises if the sun comes out and exposes the frost-covered growth to strong sunlight. This generally occurs in late spring when we assume the damage of frost is past. As soon as the situation is observed, wash the frost off with a hose. The freezing will not hurt the branch of mature foliage, but tender growth may suffer.

# 13. *Pest Control*

Most problems that arise from insect pests and disease can be controlled with two or three insecticide and fungicide sprayings in the spring at two week intervals and, again, the last week of June. In contrast to plants growing in the ground, the daily watering of bonsai will wash away many pests before they get a chance to do their damage. This applies particularly to white fly and spider mite infestations but, despite forceful water spraying, infestations may occur.

**Timing the control.**    There are two schools of thought about when to spray. One theory advocates spraying before pests appear. Except for gypsy moth and tent caterpillar, which are seasonal, there is little warning about many others. Another school suggests spraying only when needed which, in many cases, may be too late to avoid insect damage. The other drawback is that beneficial insects may also be eliminated in the process (ladybugs vs. aphid, for example) which may remove the predators as well as the enemies—and this may exacerbate an infestation that may not even have become serious in the first place.

The solution is a compromise: If there is an economic factor in cultivation, spray in advance. If the experience in your area does not suggest serious infestations, wait until pests appear. Then, if damage is observed, spray specifically for the invader. There are two exceptions: The first is for apple species which must be sprayed with a fruit-tree spray before leaves emerge (early March) and the regimen must be continued every two weeks through July. Suspend spray during pollination. The other exception is spraying against fungi which usually appear gradually and damage can be unsightly. Spray for fungi (fungicides) in advance of the season.

The best time to use insecticides is in late afternoon when the air is still. Apply the solution to bonsai stands and benches and to adjacent ground area, as well. As for equipment, it is easier and more efficient to use a portable pressure-type hand sprayer rather than spray nozzles on hose attachments. Hose-end sprayers are handy if many bonsai are to be protected, but there is a lot of waste and it is difficult to be selective when bonsai are displayed close together. Pressure-type hand sprayers enable you to focus the spray where you want it. Also, it is easier to accomplish more thorough coverage beneath leaves and reduce the risk of over-dosing. Proportional sprayers are convenient because they require no pre-mixing of concentrates. Simply fill the sprayer bottle with concentrate and set the dial for the correct dilution.

Instructions for using insecticides on package labels invariably apply to plants growing in the ground where excess chemicals are widely and harmlessly dispersed. In the confined environments of bonsai containers, over-dosing may present a risk. Apply sprays where needed and stop as soon as run-off is evident.

**Spraying precautions.**    Always wear gloves, long sleeves and protective slacks. Follow label instructions and precautions and spray only for the plant species indicated in the package labeling. Label instructions sometimes are ambiguous when identifying plant varieties for which a certain spray is applicable. Seldom do package instructions mention "bonsai" as a spraying target although instructions referring to "house plants" are common. Obviously, bonsai are not "house plants." When in doubt, follow spraying instructions for "ornamentals" or "trees and shrubs."

Most label warnings have to do with spraying fruits and vegetables for human consumption and time lapses are provided as a precaution against toxicity. Obviously, these factors do not apply for bonsai. Other warnings concern toxicity to fish and wildlife in treated areas and contamination of water supplies. These warnings, too, are of little concern to bonsai growers due to the small quantities of sprays used compared with the extensive spraying programs in commercial operations.

Nevertheless, apply just enough spray material to cover. More is never better. Clean spray equipment thoroughly after each use to prevent corrosion and contamination with other spray materials.

If you have just a few bonsai, an all-purpose aerosol spray will be suitable. Be sure to maintain adequate distance from the foliage when you release the spray from aerosols. The pressurized vehicle comes out very cold and, on hot days, this sudden contrast may be harmful. A simple, unpressurized hand sprayer works well with a few plants, but it is often difficult to calculate accurately the water dilutions for small quantities. It is better to formulate a gallon of material and sacrifice any surplus if not needed.

**Three pest types.**   We are concerned in bonsai essentially with three types of pests: (1) sucking insects which nourish themselves on plant juices, (2) chewing insects that gobble foliage and leave telltale evidence with perforated leaves and, (3) fungi that feed on plant tissue. The suckers are aphids, mealy bugs, spider mites, white fly, lace bugs and scale insects plus the pests that feed inside plant tissue such as borers and leaf miners; the chewers principally are gypsy moth, tent caterpillars and Japanese beetles; fungi, while not insects or spiders, make foliage unsightly, commonly infest apples and elms and can cause serious damage by rendering the leaves unable to function.

**Insecticide types.**   There are two kinds of insecticides to take care of the chewers and the suckers, *contact* and *systemic* sprays. Contact insecticides work when the insect feeds; the internal or systemic sprays are taken up by the roots of plants and absorbed through the foliage as contrasted to the contact sprays which remain on leaf surfaces until washed away.

Some systemics work by attacking insects when they attempt to suck a plant's juices; other systemics work by absorption into the insect's body wherein the poison is transmitted internally through the legs. Systemics cannot be washed away and often remain effective for weeks. Insects of concern to bonsai growers that can be controlled through systemics are aphids, lace bugs, leafhoppers, spider mites and white flies.

"Broad spectrum" insecticides such as Spectrocide (diazinon), Isotox and Orthene take care of the chewers, suckers and borers, plus some scale insects and mites. They are fortified with both contact and systemic chemicals which remain effective for relatively long periods of time. Hence, they need be used only when evidence of infestation is apparent.

Fungus invasions cannot be controlled with conventional insecticides. They require a specific fungicide such as captan or benylate for control. Some formulations, such as fruit-tree sprays, combine all controls—insecticides, miticides and fungicides.

**Dormant oil sprays.**   In addition to the contact and systemic sprays, the miticides and the fungicides, dormant oil is another means to control pest invasions when used at the proper time and for the correct organisms. Unfortunately, dormant oil applications have not come into popular use for bonsai. The reason, perhaps, may be that the material must be applied when plants are in the dormant stage and many enthusiasts are just not yet ready to start thinking about preventive measures. Nevertheless, emulsified oil spray, prepared from light petroleum oil, is safe, virtually non-toxic and easy to use.

Dormant oil should be used on deciduous plant species exclusively and only when bonsai are defoliated. The material works physically on over-wintering insect species such as scale, mite, aphid eggs and mealybugs by smothering the organism with a thin film of oil. There is no advantage in adding an insecticide such as malathion to dormant oil because insects are not yet active when a dormant spray should be used, although package labeling suggests this procedure on some citrus species and many nurserymen follow the practice.

It is important to remember that dormant oil should be used before leaves emerge—late February or early in March—before any new growth is evident. Apply only to the point of run-off and cover the pots with plastic sheeting to avoid contact with the soil. The plastic will also keep the pots from spotting. In situations where bonsai are wintered in garages, cool greenhouses or cold frames, the bonsai should be removed from protection, sprayed out in the open and replaced under protection to complete the season. When bonsai are wintered outdoors, there is no problem and spraying with dormant oil can be done at any time before buds break. To avoid spraying, dormant oil may also be brushed on the trunk and branches for scale control. Dilute according to the package label.

Finally, if you prefer to avoid pesticides entirely, special soaps for insect control are now available and are relatively harmless—except for the insects they exterminate. A soap spray can also be home-made with a heavy solution of a strong soap, such as Fels Naptha soap. (See page 106, "Insecticidal Soap.")

It is a rare bonsai that escapes some kind of infestation at one time or another during the growing season. Since invasions are readily seen through daily observation of our trees, pests generally are eliminated before they have had a chance to do much damage which, in most cases, simply involves a few fallen or deformed leaves. Forceful daily spraying also repels many of the most insidious pests such as aphid and spider mite. Tenacious caterpillars, however, will have to be hand picked away or eliminated with an insecticide. Persistent scale and mealy bug will have to be controlled in the early stages of development with a single dormant oil application applied in early spring when the hard, protective shells have not yet formed.

Except for a fungicide, a single broad-spectrum, all-purpose spray will suffice for most pests encountered in bonsai. Some, however, consider the broad-spectrum types too drastic because they kill almost everything that crawls or flies, often eliminating those insects that are beneficial, too. For those who wish to use specific controls, the following guidelines may be helpful:

**Gypsy moths, tent caterpillars.**   These are among the most voracious of chewing pests. Their favorite bonsai species are maples, fruit trees and some coniferous species such as pines. The specifics are Sevin (carbaryl) or malathion. The best time to spray for the "chewers" is when leaves have reached 50% of full size or when you see them suspended as tiny larvae on a web strand from trees overhead. For maples, it is best to hand-pick the pests away. Do not spray Japanese maple with anything when in full leaf. The leaves will spot and some branches may defoliate.

**Spider mites.** These tiny spiders, almost microscopic, attack a variety of plant species, especially juniper, spruce and broadleaf species. They can cause considerable damage before they are even suspected. Badly infested plants should be isolated from the rest of the collection until the infestation is under control. Malathion is the standard remedy, but Kelthane is a specific miticide. Mites can over-winter in protected areas of a plant, so a spraying in autumn is a good preventive measure. Since mites can build up an immunity to less effective controls, sprays should be alternated.

**Aphids.** These are among the sucking insects and their presence generally is not recognized until damage is apparent. If ants are present around the bonsai, you can be sure that aphids are there, too. Ants capture aphids and "milk" them for the exudate. Aphids usually attack new plant growth on the undersides of leaves. As they suck juice, the leaves crinkle, curve and stick together. Malathion is the specific. Spray at 10-day intervals.

**Mealybugs, scales.** These pests are in the same class as sucking insects. They lurk in leaf axils and the backs of leaves and excrete a sticky substance which attracts other insects and forms a medium for fungi. For local infestations, use a cotton swab dipped in rubbing alcohol. Repeat every few days. For general infestations, Cygon and malathion are the specifics.

**Fruit tree pests.** Flowering crabapple, apple and other fruiting species are susceptible to infestation and disease from the time leaves emerge to almost the end of the season. A dormant oil spray is the first line of attack followed by a fungicide until flower petals start to open. After petal fall, a fruit-tree spray containing controls for insects, mites and fungi should be used every two weeks, or more frequently if pests are present, until the end of summer.

**Oystershell scale.** Apples and other fruiting species are especially susceptible to this scale. It has a hard covering shaped like an oyster, hence its name. The covering is brownish gray, one-eighth inch long and one-sixteenth inch wide. The scale itself is yellow and soft-bodied.

Scale eggs pass the winter under the coverings of female scales. The eggs hatch in May or June and the nymphs become adult scales by mid-July. Apply a dormant oil spray before plant growth begins in the spring and spray only before new growth emerges. Where infestations of oystershell scale are heavy, follow with malathion or Cygon while the young are crawling and before the hard covering protects them.

**Fungi (blackspot).** Elm and apple varieties are especially susceptible to fungus attack and an early spring application of a fungicide will control the first onslaught. Benylate and captan are the fungicides of choice. Do not use fungicides on pines as they may destroy the beneficial soil fungus, mycorrhizae.

**Apple scab.** Another fungus that infests the leaves and twigs of apple varieties is apple scab. It starts early in the season, usually during March or early April, and remains present all summer unless caught before it proliferates. The disease appears on leaves as dark green, velvety spots which change color to brown. An early fungicide application is essential for control.

**Powdery mildew.** This is a common fungus disease that attacks apple species in humid areas. The bonsai usually survives without much damage, but the leaves become unsightly. It is characterized by a white, moldy growth that disfigures the leaves and stems. A fungicide is the prescription.

**Cedar apple rust.** A fungus disease that originates on Eastern red cedar (juniper) and is transferred to apple varieties. The disease appears first as yellow spots on the upper surfaces of leaves which soon enlarge and turn orange with black specks at the centers. Severely infected leaves become distorted and fall from the plant. Apples within a mile of the host species (Eastern red cedar) are susceptible. A fungicide is the answer.

**Fire blight.** This is a bacterial disease that attacks susceptible varieties of flowering crabapple. Some varieties are immune. Infected leaves turn brown or black, eventually dry up and remain attached to the branch.

**Forewarnings.** Do not apply insecticides to plants that are stressed. Plants should be growing actively. Avoid spraying under hot, sunny conditions. Do not spray under humid conditions, when it is too cool or when the bonsai will not dry out quickly. Don't spray when the bonsai are in need of water. Wilted or dry plants are vulnerable to injury. If parts of a plant appear to have been burned, if spotting or yellowing occurs, if leaves curl or otherwise appear to be mis-shapen— you may suspect insecticide damage.

**Checking for spider mite.** Infestation during September and October is common. You can spot them by holding a white card under branches and tapping them lightly. If mites are present, you will see them moving around. Junipers and spruces are commonly the victims.

**Repelling rodents.** To keep squirrels and birds from disturbing soil surfaces in their search for grubs, surround the plantings with creosoted rope which may be purchased at garden centers as "Dog and Cat Repellent." Position the rope along bench edges, not on the pots. Creosote, in contact with foliage, is poisonous. When applied at a cold pit to repel mice, string the rope along an outside perimeter. Napthalene moth balls also repel rodents as long as they can be kept dry.

**Protective spraying, indoor bonsai.** Spray for insect pests and fungi before bonsai are brought indoors or put away for the winter at the end of the growing season and spray, again, when bonsai are brought out of winter protection. Many pests, such as spider mite, scale and fungi winter over on woody parts of the plants. They resume activity at the first sign of spring outdoors.

**Avoiding trouble.** Bonsai should never be subjected to any kind of stress that may retard growth. Stress can be a result of inadequate watering and root disease is caused by overwatering. Infestations undermine the health of any plant and certain plant species under water stress will be susceptible to spider mite, too. Bonsai growers who do not allow their plants to be under stress for whatever the reason will have the fewest problems with insects and disease.

**Covering ground cover.** To keep blue jays and other curious birds away from moss, place squares of half-inch or quarter-inch wire fencing material over the soil surface. Once they get the idea, the barriers can be removed.

**Nuisance pest.** Rock plantings fed with small quantities of dried fertilizer may attract sowbugs or pillbugs. These peculiar little animals are not insects at all, but crustaceans like the millipedes. They apparently do no damage since they feed on decaying material in the moss and in the soil. They are about half-an-inch long with segmented bodies. Some species roll up and look like "pills" when disturbed. They like damp environments and decaying material and are very common under plants kept on wood benches. Spectrocide, used sparingly, will keep the creatures under control.

**Bugs away.** To keep crawlers, including ants, away from your benches, apply a product called Tanglefoot. It is used on trees to trap caterpillars and may be purchased at nurseries. Paint a strip around the legs of your benches and the bugs won't be able to get past it.

**Yellowing junipers.** If junipers start to turn yellow despite a consistent fertilizing schedule, this could mean any of three things: (1) iron deficiency which can be corrected with an iron-fortified fertilizer or Sequestrine, (2) low soil pH which makes it impossible for the plant to absorb the nutrients in the fertilizer and, (3) infestation by spider mite. The last reason is usually the least cause for suspicion because the mites are not apparent until the damage is done. These tiny creatures feed by sucking sap from leaf tissue. Junipers are a favorite target for these pests and late summer infestations are common. A prophylactic spraying in autumn with a specific miticide such as Kelthane before bonsai are winterized will prevent over-wintering pests from taking over again in the spring.

**Pest control through watering.** A daily application of a forceful stream of water usually removes many insect pests that otherwise could cause appreciable damage to foliage. A strong hosing will break up webs of spider mites, wash away aphids and interrupt egg-laying activities of other pests. Unfortunately, watering also removes natural predators such as ladybug, praying mantis, green lacewings and beneficial spiders. Of course, discretion should be used as to the actual "force" of a forceful spray to avoid breaking branches and leaves on tender stock.

**Insecticidal soap.** Soap has proven to be an ally in the battle against susceptible insects. This relatively new product was developed by a Canadian entomologist and is marketed under the name of Safer Insecticidal Soap. It is the only soap developed exclusively for plant use. For effective control, it must be applied frequently. Since soap is alkaline, however, it should not be overused on plant species that prefer acid soil such as azalea as it may reduce the acid level. To play safe, cover the soil before application and remove the cover after the insecticide has dried.

**Search and destroy.** Close inspection before plants are watered frequently reveals the presence of caterpillars, inch worms, leaf rollers and other voracious pests. Picking them off and destroying them is an effective control, but there are some the eye can't see such as spider mites. Only after discoloration of foliage has occurred do we suspect infestation. For a major invasion, chemical insecticides are the only alternative.

Malathion is considered the least hazardous insecticide to humans and plants and it is effective against a wide range of insects that are a concern to bonsai growers among which are mealybug, scale crawlers and aphids. Kelthane, alternated with malathion, is best for mites. It has been reported that some mite species have become resistant to malathion. Hidden or hard to reach insects are best controlled with systemics.

**Spraying maples.** Aphids are the most common nuisance that infest Japanese maples and trident maples. Conventional sprays will spot the leaves, make them unsightly, and, often, cause them to drop off. Use insecticidal soap. This takes care of the pest without leaf damage. Repeated applications are required. When ants are observed crawling around the leaves and twigs of maples, look for aphids in the crotches.

**Weather and infestations.**    Insect populations proliferate during periods of heavy rainfall and reduce in population during hot, dry conditions. For example, apple scab shows up as discolored leaves. The disease thrives when a film of moisture remains on leaves for several hours.

On the other hand, seasons of low precipitation and moderate temperatures contribute to a higher incidence of some insects. Aphids thrive during these periods. Since they are soft-bodied insects (plant lice), they are inhibited by hot, dry weather and thrive during periods of high humidity and moisture.

Spider mites also increase in population during long, dry spells. They can complete their life cycles within a week. As the population on a plant intensifies, a fine webbing will be apparent.

Caterpillar infestations come in cycles. Several seasons can pass with very little evidence of their presence. Suddenly, there may be an onslaught of gypsy moth and tent caterpillars and, when the population becomes overwhelming, protective measures should be taken.

# 14. *Indoor Bonsai*

The word "indoor" for bonsai often is misleading when it comes to selecting material for indoor cultivation. Since bonsai are portable and so easy to move around, many individuals feel they can be kept indoors like houseplants. Except for very short periods of time, a day or two at the most, conventional material which thrives outdoors cannot be brought inside unless environmentally conditioned for survival.

Most species of true houseplants started out in the tropics which makes them suitable for cultivation in an indoor environment. In contrast, plant material typically grown for bonsai is genetically conditioned for outdoor cultivation. Unfortunately, there are no plant species for specific cultivation indoors as bonsai analogous to those varieties which are used for houseplants. *Houseplants* and *indoor bonsai* are separate areas of container-grown culture.

However, many bonsai species can be adapted to houseplant conditions. Tropicals such as gardenia and buttonwood usually present no problem. Podocarpus, Kingsville box, serissa and others of dubious hardiness outdoors are favorites for indoor cultivation if they are given correct and often critical conditions of light, humidity and temperature requirements, both warmth and cold. Indeed, even the popular coniferous and deciduous species can be developed as "indoor" bonsai if they are permitted a period of dormancy for four or five weeks in a protected area outdoors or, indoors, in a refrigerator.

Such typical bonsai species grown indoors do best where the light is best. This usually translates into an east or a west window. A south window is suitable if shaded by a sheer curtain to diffuse the light and prevent burn. Weak, spindly growth usually can be traced to inadequate light.

**The requisites.** The great advantage of indoor cultivation is the complete control one enjoys over the plant's environment and the subsequent adaptation to human living conditions. Light is the easiest element to control. It is difficult for the human eye to make an accurate evaluation to the contrast between the light available indoors and out, but when this contrast is measured scientifically and designated in "foot candles," there is a considerable difference.

For the sake of contrast, bright sunlight outdoors amounts to 10,000 such units of foot candles and 5,000 foot candles in a shaded area, whereas light reflected from a wall opposite a bright window in a living room may measure as little as 50. It stands to reason that very few growing things can endure that measure of light exposure. On a windowsill with south, east or west exposure, a natural light value of 1,000 foot candles can be measured, but this is still a long way from the amount of light available outdoors for bonsai kept even in the shadiest locations.

In addition to "low light tolerant" varieties suitable for bonsai styling, such as chrysanthemum, azalea and other woody flowering species, there is also a direct relationship between leaf size and the amount of light required. The smaller the leaf, the more light needed.

**The light solution.** In order to compensate for a natural light deficiency with those plant species that require more than a bright windowsill and correct direction exposure, fluorescent lamps are the only solution. The only disadvantage of this supplemental light requisite is that plants must be isolated from the rest of the house. It is difficult to incorporate an elaborate arrangement within the living quarters. A basement area or spare room where complete temperature control is available is ideal.

Also, unless the artificial light source is very close to the plant, the system becomes inefficient. Two standard white fluorescent lamps placed six inches from the plants deliver about 860 foot candles to the foliage and this should be the minimum. This drops to 500 at twelve inches and to about 380 at eighteen inches.

Longer light exposure can be used to compensate for the lower light intensity at farther distances, but there also is the need for a rest period of darkness. Eighteen hours of artifical light usually is the maximum any plant can endure. Plants also can be turned periodically to spread available illumination, but this often presents a problem in large plant material and an extensive collection.

Next comes the matter of temperature. High temperatures and low light can cause excessive foliage growth. While this feature is not an objection in conventional house plants, it is a distinct disadvantage in bonsai.

The less light a plant receives, the lower the temperature should be kept. There should be a 10° difference at least between daytime and nighttime temperatures. A drop at night to the 50's would be adequate with an average between 65° and 70° during daylight hours.

**Moisture requirements.** The next factor is humidity. Most living quarters are notoriously low in air moisture. The amount of humidity usually available indoors can simulate desert conditions which, except for cacti, is intolerable for most species used for bonsai, indoors or out. This dryness can be corrected partially through the daily use of a household humidifier and through supplemental mistings several times a day.

Setting the plants on trays of gravel beds in water will create an aura of humidity in the area close to the plants. The brighter the light, the more humidity plants will require. Sand is not an efficient bed for the pots to rest on. The pots will sink in, whereas pebbles or gravel will support the pots just above the water surface. Peat moss presents the same disadvantage as sand and it is messy to have around. Plastic "egg crate" grids known as light diffusers can be cut to size and placed over the beds to keep the water from contact with the pots.

Pots on pebbles in water won't exactly saturate the air with moisture other than the immediate vicinity of the plants, but the humidity environment will be greatly improved. Many orchid fanciers keep these tropicals alive and healthy through the micro-environment created with this simple device—beds of pebbles or gravel covered with water just below the pebble surfaces. Of course, fresh water will have to be added to the pans from time to time.

Water evaporation occurs only from the water surface in contact with the air, not the depth of water in the trays. The water evaporation area can be increased by floating wood shavings on the water to multiply the number of evaporation surfaces exposed to the air. The thicker the shavings and the more the curl, the better they will serve as evaporators. If you don't mind the appearance, accordian-folded strips of blotting paper can also be used for this purpose. With a correct watering regimen and moderate humidity measures, moisturization requirements will be fulfilled.

**Controlling algae.** When indoor bonsai are placed over pans of water to moisturize the air, surface algae often develop. This is unsightly and, when algae build-up becomes heavy, it can reduce water evaporation. To reduce algae formation, for each gallon of water in the trays add an ounce of Clorox plus a few pinches of synthetic detergent ("All"). This will keep the water fresh for long periods, even after new water is added to compensate for evaporation, but pebbles and trays will have

to be subjected to a thorough cleansing every few months.

Watering is the last of the indoor bonsai requisites. In situations of strong, adequate light, high room temperatures and low humidity, frequent watering will be required.

Finally, cultural care will be necessary the same as for bonsai grown outdoors. Since the growing season is longer indoors, more pinching and pruning will be needed and fertilizing will have to be attended to with regularity. Also, control from insect pests will be the same as for outdoor care, but spraying insecticides indoors should be avoided for human safety.

Experienced growers of houseplants will find it easy to make the transition to indoor bonsai cultivation once suitable environments are created. Greenhouse conditions of light, heat and humidity should be duplicated as closely as possible.

Most growers transfer indoor-grown bonsai to the out-of-doors for the summer. This can be hazardous to the health of the plant, however, due to the extreme contrast in light exposure. Obviously, full sun should be avoided. Even in deep shade, the amount of light contrasted with indoor availability may be too much for the plant to endure.

What is more, if a plant accustomed to indoors is successful in negotiating the outside growing conditions for a short summer season, it will have to cope with a low-light environment indoors when ultimately restored to the indoor winter quarters. With a prized specimen, the requisite for drastically changing the environment is vigilance.

**Large material indoors.** The cultivation of indoor bonsai under lights needn't be confined to scrawny, small material that looks "pretty" when grouped with African violets and begonia. Large material can be successfully handled, too.

The author has kept under lights from October through April a large podocarpus with a four inch trunk at the base that stands forty inches from container rim to apex and thirty inches across from the widest branch tips.

The tree was maintained in a basement corner below a slightly opened window. The inside temperatures ranged from 66° to 70° during the day and lower at night. It was surrounded with cool-white fluorescents, forty-eight inches long. Two fixtures, with double tubes, were suspended from the ceiling and two more fixtures, each with double tubes, were set on the floor *vertically*. This represented eight 48-inch lights in all. Very little light came through the small window and the fluorescents were kept on fourteen hours a day.

The lights were only inches away from the foliage. The pot, set on gravel/water pans, rested on a turntable so the tree could be rotated a quarter-turn daily. In this way, top and sides got equal light distribution for most of a one-week period.

The tree was watered two or three times a week and

only when the soil surface was dry to the touch. To keep water from running off the dry soil surface at watering times, the soil was sprayed for a few seconds before water was applied. This decreased surface tension and enabled the water to soak through the root ball quickly and run through the bottom to the gravel bed below. From May through October, the tree was summered outdoors in filtered sun after a two-week period in shade— and it did exhibit some resentment to the contrast from indoor to outdoor exposure.

When plants are exposed to inadequate light intensity indoors, they will not perform well in spite of correct temperature and humidity levels. If the natural light is too intense for species that thrive in low light conditions, leaves will wilt and turn yellow and dry areas will develop on the foliage. When there is too little light, older leaves will drop and new growth will be weak.

**Light Intensifier.** To increase daylight on indoor bonsai kept on a window sill, set up a piece of white cardboard inside the room the width of the window and at an angle that reflects the light from the outside. A little trial and error will indicate the correct angle to catch the most daylight and bounce it back to the plant. Professional photographers use white cardboard all the time to remove shadows and brighten an area.

**Light conditioning.** Bonsai conditioned to indoor environment often are brought outdoors for the summer. It makes sense to keep them in partial sun. Even the most intense light indoors is but a fraction of the light outdoors. In addition, they should be exposed gradually from deep shade to filtered sun. A summer of full sun exposure might be too much.

Conversely bonsai brought in from the outdoors after a summer of natural light exposure should be placed in shade for about two weeks before the transition. Also, it seems logical to bring them in before the house heat comes up in the temperate areas of the country. Air dryness and low light are the biggest contrasts in restoring indoor cultivation to bonsai summered outdoors.

**Indoor sabbatical.** Bonsai species that cannot endure hard winters (Kingsville box, Catlin elm, Serissa) can be brought in as *indoor bonsai* after they have been exposed to a short period of cold outdoors (four or five weeks). They can be pruned, wired and fertilized when new growth becomes apparent and returned outdoors again after frost danger has passed.

**Artificial light arrangements.** High wattage (150 watts) incandescent lights placed four feet directly above foliage provides adequate intensity. Fluorescent light can be located closer to the plant to provide higher light intensity. Because fluorescent light produces less heat than incandescent light, heat damage to plants does not occur. A typical installation requires two 40-watt fluorescent tubes twelve inches above the plants. Such a setup provides minimum light requirements. A four-tube fixture, or two 2-tube fixtures set side by side, doubles the light intensity and is adequate for flowering plants and woody species.

**Controlling insects indoors.** Wash leaves with soapy water, use insecticidal soap spray or an insect spray registered for indoor use. Take plants to the garage or a shady spot outdoors when spraying with anything stronger. Small "Whisper Fans" are available at horticultural supply centers and are used by professional growers to keep mold and fungi under control by supplying air movement.

**Gift bonsai and houseplants.** Bonsai received as gifts or acquired by personal purchase often get into trouble because the new owner may be unfamiliar with basic care and culture needs. Usually, these acquisitions are looked upon as houseplants and are commonly kept indoors. This could be a bonsai disaster.

The problem arises when the new owner does not realize that many bonsai produced for over-the counter sale are styled from outdoor-woodland plants that have a rigid set of genetic requirements, rather than from species that can safely be grown indoors.

Species such as maples, elms, pines and junipers— even apple varieties—are conditioned to severe outdoor environments of temperature and humidity, including prolonged exposure to cold during dormancy. These deciduous and coniferous species need every element of exposure found only out-of-doors such as sunlight, cool nights and air circulation. Indoor growing conditions are hostile to such species.

Bonsai styled from deciduous and coniferous stock and kept indoors for a prolonged period of time, without proper conditioning, soon peter out. When they fail, it becomes a bitter disappointment. This is a bonsai fact of life that many people do not realize.

On the other hand, gifts of bonsai styled form traditional outdoor species can be enjoyed on a sunny terrace or patio without corrective measures for survival.

Finally, gift bonsai styled form plants that can thrive in indoor environments with a correct balance of temperature and humidity as previously described, encounter no problems. Plants such as serissa, podocarpus, boxwood varieties—even azalea, buttonwood and gardenia when procured from Southern U.S. areas— can do well indoors with normal care and culture.

Deciduous plants and conifers, however, when kept indoors, are programmed for failure. This dilemma usually occurs when a well-intentioned gift-giver—and the recipient, as well—are strangers to bonsai care and culture.

# 15. *Displaying Bonsai*

**Sharing bonsai.** A bonsai hobbyist acquiring or creating a bonsai invariably desires another and, perhaps, another—always aiming for the perfect specimen until, in time, he finds himself with a "collection." These are the symptoms of the syndrome. To be fully enjoyed, bonsai cannot be contemplated alone. Bonsai must be shared. That is one of the reasons for displaying them in public. Pride of ownership is strong and fanciers rightfully want to "show off" their creations to others.

The appreciation of bonsai is not a "do-it-yourself" proposition. If you simply want to contemplate a tree in solitude without the pleasure of sharing it with someone else, then almost any setting will do. But if your bonsai are to be admired by friends, family or neighbors, then more thought must be devoted to the window dressing.

If the practitioner has only one or two good specimens, they usually are pampered and petted. They are carefully installed on a choice spot on the patio, terrace or apartment balcony where they can be admired by the owner during periods of relaxation, or bonsai can be brought indoors, if the plants are outdoor material, for an occasional sojourn on the dining room table to be praised by dinner guests. The object is the same: a place is set aside where they can be enjoyed by the owner and others.

**Why display.** For the serious hobbyist, however, there is more to it than merely courting the admiration of others. Bonsai become like pets in a family; they require care, perhaps daily surveillance, plus a convenient place to administer to their needs for training and a place protected from the extreme elements of sun, shade, wind and rain.

So they must be displayed. And displaying bonsai constitutes a presentation. This may be for the purpose of education, at home and at institutional exhibits, in competition, or for personal and private enjoyment of the creator.

The center of interest in Japanese sitting rooms usually is the tokonoma, a beautifully-carved multi-leveled stand where miniature bonsai, usually indoor species, are permanently set in place. Much thought and attention is devoted to the placement of these bonsai. Those of the same height are not placed adjacent to one another, nor are conifer species mixed with deciduous in the same proximity. Branches pointing outward are never situated at the ends of displays because that would tend to lead the eye away from the picture. Likewise, bonsai with curved or slanting trunks are placed so the eye travels into the picture rather than away from it.

The traditional Japanese tokonoma is six or nine feet long, two feet deep and two to five inches above the floor. Shelves are of varied lengths and heights. Some tokonoma are elaborately carved and elegantly finished and polished and constructed of exotic woods.

**For display outdoors.** The best environment for outdoor species is a special place in the yard, away from a wall that may reflect too much light or impede air circulation. This setup can be as simple as a single shelf or as complex as a major construction project involving benches of varying heights, plinths, stands and pedestals. Bonsai should never be displayed directly under a roof or low-hanging tree, or one specimen behind another. Each one must be set for maximum visibility without competition from an adjacent planting.

If a large number of bonsai are arranged on long shelves, they should be zig-zagged so each tree is exposed to adequate light and air. Avoid the feeling of a straight line.

Ideally, large bonsai should be displayed low, approximately two feet off the ground. Smaller bonsai should be displayed approximately at table height on stands about thirty inches from the ground.

Stand widths should be about three feet wide, utilizing a double plank, for an interesting arrangement. Trees of the same height should be separated for contrast. For a change of pace, individual stands, randomly positioned, can be used to emphasize special specimens. A ground cover of pebbles or crushed rock can be placed under the stand for weed control and drainage of surplus water.

In short, the display of bonsai can be likened to the planning of a garden. If it entices the viewer to come in and browse around, it has served its purpose. Finally, if bonsai is like a work of art and the pot is like the frame of a picture, then display can be considered the packaging. A good package may not necessarily improve a poor product, but it certainly gets the idea across.

**Display benches and stands.** There are various methods for elevating the stands off the ground. As mentioned above, large bonsai should be displayed two feet high and small bonsai just below eye level, although this is a relative dimension depending on the height of the viewer.

Logs, ten to twelve inches in diameter, make a rustic under-carriage for the shelves. The logs should be treated with wood preservative to avoid decay in contact with the ground as should the planks on top of them. The logs can also be set on flagstones or concrete slabs to avoid ground contact. On freshly cut logs, the bark will be retained for several years, after which it will fall away and the cambium surface eventually will take on an attractive driftwood appearance.

If wood preservative is replenished from time to time after the bark falls away, the logs will last for many years and improve in appearance as time goes on. The author has used about twenty such logs for undercarriage for more than twelve years and while there are some signs of decay, they are still solid and serviceable.

Ceramic flue pots, used in chimney construction and available at building supply centers, make excellent undercarriages for shelves. They come in standard lengths of thirty inches and have square or rectangular shapes. Some are available in an attractive earthy color while others are a subdued light beige. These flue pots, too, are subject to destruction in contact with the ground due to freezing and thawing, but they remain serviceable for long periods of time.

Another option for the undercarriage support of shelves are 4″ × 4″ legs, also treated with wood preservative, and sunk 1-½ feet below the ground. A post hole digger is the tool to use for this purpose. These 4″ x 4″ legs present a more formal appearance and much more work is involved to level them for uniform height.

**Cement block bases.** Common cement blocks, either solid or open molded, are ideal bases for planks and once leveled and set in place, are practically permanent. Cement blocks also are available in attractive designs but, in large quantity, they become overpowering compared with the simple appearance of the standard shapes.

Once the base material is decided upon, the next consideration is the choice of planks. Pressure-treated lumber, two inches thick and approximately ten inches wide, is preferred. If finished lumber is used, the two inches becomes slightly more than 1-¾ inch. Unfinished stock is ideal if it is available.

For a small bonsai collection, a simple structure of cement blocks and two ten-inch planks side by side and ten feet long, will usually suffice. Three undercarriage stands for this length should be used to avoid a dip in the center, although the stands may be placed closer together with heavier bonsai positioned over the supports. An embellishment of this would be four ten-inch planks attached with 2″ × 4″ cross pieces to make the total width approximately 42″ so the bonsai can be staggered on the bench rather than displayed side by side. See photos, pages 113, 114.

**For special effect.** To accent outstanding specimens and for a change of pace in displaying bonsai, free-standing plinths or pedestals can be erected by arranging cement blocks side by side two or three layers high. A finished base for these individual pedestals can be accomplished by setting the cement blocks on 4″ thick cement block slabs which, like the cement blocks themselves, can be purchased inexpensively at building supply centers.

Once you have decided on the use of cement blocks and observe the various assortments available, different combinations will come to mind for maximum utility and attractiveness. Two-tier arrangements are also possible by setting blocks on edges above the double-plank design to create a single shelf above the two adjacent ones. This upper elevation is ideal for the smallest bonsai, situated, as they are, at or just above eye level.

Benches should be placed on the north-south axis for full sun situations and east-west for partial shading. For more shade, one end of the arrangement can be positioned under a tall tree if special attention is devoted to keeping the area free of debris and insect pests.

**Decent exposure.** In order for all bonsai to receive uniform sunlight coverage, turn the pots 90° once a week. You may not always have the front of the tree in the most choice location, but the change of exposure will be beneficial. For large bonsai which are difficult to handle, the pots may be set on inexpensive plastic turntables which may be purchased at most variety stores.

**Benefits of morning sunlight.** Turgidity in plants is suspended long before twilight and it is re-established at the first rays of morning sunlight. If you have a choice of morning or afternoon sun exposure, pick morning. The first light of dawn is the most important of the day. It also hastens evaporation of night-time moisture accumulation.

**How to get your bonsai ready for exhibit.** When you are invited to participate in a show, certain preparations must be planned in advance before putting your bonsai on display.

Bonsai are traditionally exhibited on mats or stands to separate the planting from the table surface. Grass cloth mats cut in proportion to the container size are perfect. Inexpensive "breakfast" mats can be purchased at many housewares counters, but the colors and patterns should be neutral and inconspicuous.

To make your bonsai presentable for exhibit, eliminate dead leaves and branches. Clean up the soil surface. Clean the outside of the container with a damp cloth and, to impart a finished gloss, polish with baby oil or mineral oil. Remove moss if discolored and replace with fresh moss. Remove heavy wiring. Moderate and inconspicuous wiring generally is acceptable. Water the soil thoroughly before presenting the bonsai for display and allow time for drainage before placing them on location.

*Suitable display benches can be set up on concrete blocks with 2″ × 4″ cross pieces supporting 2″ × 10″ planks 12-feet long paired for display on each side. Total width of each display side is 19 inches with a 2-1/2″ space between each side.*

*Separate plinths can be arranged with cement blocks for displaying individual specimens, as shown.*

*Flue pots 8″ × 12-½″ and 24-inches tall can be used for a single display bench with two 2″ × 10″ planks side by side.*

# 16. *Collecting Bonsai*

For the purpose of styling plant material into bonsai, nothing can duplicate the rugged and natural look of plants growing in the wild compared with "domesticated" material purchased from nurseries, cultivated for garden use and landscaping, balled and bagged or grown in cans in wholesale quantities and artificially stimulated with fertilizers to entice the consumer.

When compared with nursery-grown stock, collected material almost always possesses that rough, aged look and other priceless qualities we strive for in styling. Driftwood, scars of adversity and naturally contorted trunks and branches deliver a communication of genuine age because they are aged—the same illusion we try to achieve through artificial means.

While the ground rules of bonsai styling are much easier to administer in the case of nursery-grown material where we have a larger assortment of branching to work with, the naturalness of collected specimens compensates for the lack of other elements. When styling collected material from the wild, some ground rules of design must be compromised.

The potential for development of a picturesque tree in nature, one of the goals in bonsai, is more easily accomplished with collected material.

**The contrasts.** Naturally tapered trunks, strong surface roots and an aging image are almost always the rewards of collecting because we automatically reject commercial material that lacks these qualities—whereas these traits may take years to establish in nursery-grown stock through careful selection, patience and technique.

Collecting from the wild also presents a challenge and it is a tribute to horticultural skill. It can be a great source of pleasure and satisfaction in itself and a triumph when it responds.

Permission must always be sought from a property owner or municipality before you venture into a collecting area. Violations on publicly-owned property can be serious and private property owners rightfully resent trespassers.

Digging for naturally-grown plants demands the greatest care and patience and the preservation of a good root system is the major hazard. Feeder roots sometimes reach five or six feet away from the trunk and if they are not present at all, or if they are removed in the digging process without allowing a period of re-growth, results can be hopeless. In addition, older plants in the wild lack the vigor of youth and are slow to respond and recover.

There are two methods for collecting: (1) performing the operation over two or three growing seasons and, (2) lifting material from the ground in one digging session. In each situation, the best time to perform the function is in late winter or early spring.

If the material to be collected looks old and well established and the site is readily accessible for periodic visits, the procedure should be tackled in stages.

Start with a series of root prunings. The roots should be severed within six or twelve inches from the trunk, completely cutting through all the roots encountered. Do this halfway around the base of the tree. In addition to a sharp spade, the operation may also require the use of a branch lopper and sturdy saw. One warning: Tools in contact with soil dull quickly. For root work, discarded tools are best, or some instruments for this purpose should be set aside and used only for these operations.

The next season, repeat the operation around the rest of the circle at the tree base. After a full growing season, sufficient fibrous roots will have become re-established and the ball can be prepared for lifting.

**Getting the ball out.** After the roots have been cut back and new growth has become apparent, dig a trench six inches wide from the root-pruning line outward. When the trench is completed, this will enable you to shift and raise the ball enough so you can get your hand beneath and sever the tap root, if there is one. Once the ball is free, tip it to the edge of the hole so you can lay in burlap or plastic sheeting. Then tip it the other way to complete wrapping the ball. Use the burlap or plastic as a sling to lift the ball out of the hole.

Before tightening the burlap around the ball, spray the roots. Wrap the burlap tightly around the ball, tie with twine and saturate the outside of the burlap so the ball will be moist until you get it home. If plastic is used instead of burlap, make sure the edges overlap to avoid losing moisture from the ball.

The foregoing represents the most conservative procedure for collecting a specimen from the wild. The size of the root ball can be estimated at the time of the first root pruning, but leave as large a ball as possible consistent with the weight you can carry. A full root ball, 12-inches in diameter, will weigh approximately 50 lbs. If the ball looks too heavy, scrape away a little more of the soil, especially from the top surface of the ball. But dig as large a hole as you can handle. The hardest part is lifting the ball from the hole.

**Reducing the top.**    After the first root-pruning, you can reduce the top of the specimen by cutting away all unwanted branches. This will lighten your load and also take pressure off the reduced root system. You will also have to amputate the trunk to reduce the height of the tree. This should be done just above a branch that can serve as a continuation of the trunk unless you choose to retain as much of the original trunk as possible for later styling or jinning.

Young and vigorous material can be collected and balled immediately without going through the stages above and without much survival risk. When such a likely candidate is found for collecting, and there is some evidence of fibrous roots close to the trunk, the procedure is relatively simple and safe from the standpoint of results.

Method number 2. Dig a trench around the plant starting about a foot away from the trunk. Then gradually dig inward until you have created a neat ball. If a taproot is present, carefully pass your hand below to sever it before you lift the ball. Otherwise, the ball will fall apart if the taproot is still connected to the ground. Then wrap the ball in burlap or plastic, tie tightly with twine, moisten the ball as described above and prune away unwanted material at the top. If the ball is small and tight before applying the burlap, it may be lifted out first and the burlap applied after the ball is removed from the hole. If not, it's best to take steps to keep the ball intact. The important consideration here is to avoid bare-rooting the specimen.

Remember, trees and shrubs growing in the wild do not have fibrous roots closely confined to the trunk in contrast to nursery-grown material. When not root-pruned in advance of lifting to allow fibrous roots to restore themselves, you may have to save a long feeder root to preserve the fibrous roots at the end until a new crop of fibrous roots can be grown.

It is essential to have a place ready to pot the newly collected material as soon as you return home. This may be a large pot, tub or box with adequate drainage and a soil consisting of part native material in which the specimen was growing and a generous proportion of sand, Turface or other potting medium with good drainage characteristics. The newly-collected specimen must be kept shaded until new growth is evident at which time preliminary wiring can be applied although major styling plans should wait until a full season passes in the training container.

**Potting patience.**    Don't be too eager to transplant the specimen in a conventional ceramic pot. Trees transplanted from the wild require a prolonged period to recover. Two or three repottings may be necessary before you are able to "pot down" to the desired size.

Here are other suggestions for a collecting expedition:

1. Wear clothes suitable for the outdoor wilds. A lot of work will have to be done on hands and knees, so wear clothes that won't be "spoiled" if they get soiled. Knee pads will make the job more comfortable, but they are cumbersome if you plan to do a lot of walking.

2. In addition to a spade, loppers and saw, bring a trowel or grub hoe, plastic bags, burlap, plastic sheeting, twine, pruning shears and a knapsack or duffle bag to carry the gear. Wear rubbers or waterproof shoes.

3. An antidesiccant spray will be useful to help prevent moisture transpiration on foliage plus a conventional spray bottle containing water so you won't have to search for a water supply when you need it.

4. Finally, on any collecting trip, don't overlook the opportunity to collect moss and lichen. Don't tackle specimens that appear "impossible"—leave these to Mother Nature and, finally, don't leave an unsightly, pock-marked area where the collected trees once grew. Fill in the holes with top soil from an adjacent area.

Collecting from the wild need not be an act of pillaging the environment for our own artistic desires, nor is it environmental blasphemy. It can be a worthy act of preservation and sharing with others the wondrous aspects of nature in the wild. Bonsai in pots are coddled by comparison. They can flourish in containers and live longer than those exposed to the rigors of nature.

# Epilogue

There is something about bonsai that gets into your blood. Emotional attachments appear that are hard to explain. They can get out of proportion when one considers that the object is just another living organism. But nature does not evaluate beauty among the priorities.

Even to seasoned growers, the loss of a favorite bonsai may sometimes be traumatic. There apparently exists a motivation about bonsai more complex than the mere satisfaction of nurturing a growing object. There is an inexorable reward that lies always in the future—the challenge of success—the ineffable explanation of reaching for perfection that never quite arrives. The journey thus becomes the destination.

Somehow or other, the perfection syndrome takes over. We scrupulously try to avoid overstepping the ground rules for bonsai styling, but common sense suggests that, sometimes, rules must be compromised. When we slavishly follow the rules, we often are doomed to disappointment. Ground rules should represent guidelines rather than rigid restrictions. When rules are bent, we may not possess an ultimate bonsai, but a "potted tree" can be almost as rewarding.

Bonsai is a potted tree by design—*ideal* and *picturesque*—an object studied, planned and shaped so the end result is not only a miniature tree growing in a suitable container, but also a tree growing in a container *plus* a measure of grace, beauty, proportion and harmony. The more carefully we recognize and execute the guidelines, the closer we come to the quest for the perfect tree.

Collected specimens, naturally miniaturized by nature, may violate the rules because their beauty lies in their struggle to survive despite the deprivation they endured, disadvantaged by the elements. For nursery grown plant material and trees in training, ground rule guidelines are more easily put into practice.

**The compromises.**   Wiring branches is one of the tools for bonsai styling. The rules have to do with esthetics rather than the restraining capacity of mechanical forces. Actually, a branch can be restrained just as effectively with wires crossing, which is taboo.

We also are cautioned against allowing wire to remain coiled around a branch too long to avoid surface scarring. True, this is unsightly—especially to seasoned observers. Does this spell disaster? Only esthetically. What happens to tight wire around the roots of bonsai that have been secured within the pot to hold the rootball in place? We don't see the wire, so it is forgotten.

117

Are the roots strangled? Sometimes this wire is severed from below and cut away but, more often than not, roots that have been squeezed by wire do not become useless. They simply throw out new growth at the point of injury. The damaged roots die away and disappear as new roots develop unencumbered and take over. Wire blemished branches also survive. They may look unsightly but, often, they pass unnoticed. In many ways, nature protects bonsai from ignorance or neglect.

In bonsai, we do not dwell on the past. Who can deny a feeling of triumph when a tree in training responds? Even when a tree is lost, we try to learn a lesson for the future. It's always off with the old and on with the new.

**Look for reasons of failure.**   If a plant, or even a branch, dies, do a post-mortem. Try to determine the cause. Junipers lose branches for no apparent reason. Close scrutiny, however, may reveal that one branch may have shaded another, that bark inadvertently was scraped and the branch was girdled, or vital foliage was injured. If you examine an expired branch, you may see a small break in the stem caused by wiring or rough handling.

Roots can also be rendered useless by overwatering. A soil inspection will reveal a lifeless root mass rather than crisp, white growth at the root ends exploring the potting medium.

If the soil smells dank and sour, remove the moss. It may be sodden below. Sometimes moss grows too abundantly over the soil surface like a canopy with a protected air space below which is not apparent. Moisture below the moss canopy becomes stagnant. The remedy: Remove the heavy moss covering, allow the soil surface to dry completely, then replace the moss thinly with small patches to allow more soil surface to be exposed to the air. This situation occurs most frequently in rock plantings where moss is used extensively to retain soil, especially on slanting surfaces.

Then there is the apprehensive loss of foliage. Most growers expect deciduous species to lose leaves in autumn, but they may fail to realize that the same phenomenon occurs with needled evergreens, too. They become alarmed when pine needles discolor and fall away. During September and October, the inner, older foliage of most evergreen conifers dies and drops as new needles mature.

This natural needle-casting may be contrasted with the severe needle damage caused by disease. In this situation, needle loss occurs over the whole tree as new growth discolors and falls away as well as the old.

Finally, don't be too quick to sever an azalea branch that appears to have succumbed to winter-kill. The branch may resume growth from old wood as the season develops—often, even a season later.

**The obsession with styles.**   Trends in bonsai styles run in cycles and there are those who have preferences for one style over another, such as group or rock plantings. The usual pattern among average growers is to start with a single tree. The interest gradually moves to multiple-trunk and group stylings. If one is fortunate enough to acquire a quantity of wildlings unsuitable for single-tree styles, a group planting may be the solution. Some growers develop skills for specialized presentations such as grass plantings and bonsai groups with rock outcroppings known as *Saikei* which depict miniature landscapes. There are no "specialist" stylists, however, who concentrate exclusively on formal uprights, informal uprights, slanting styles, windswept, etc. Most of the time, style decisions and variations develop as a result of the material at hand.

Some growers go to extremes in selecting stone planters and slabs that substitute for conventional pots, as well as impressively shaped rocks for rock plantings. It is common to cement rocks together to create exotic shapes. Then they are carved with planting shelves and pockets as well as serpentine curves to resemble Chinese river rocks—top heavy, ornate and statuesque enough without the addition of living bonsai.

While volcanic rock is a popular medium and relatively easy to carve compared with granite or other stony mass where specialized tools and carving chisels are required, it is not always the bed of roses portrayed in demonstrations and published descriptions.

Then there is the matter of size. The choice is closely related to available space and physical strength of the stylist.

**It doesn't have to be big to be beautiful.**    In addition to the various styles, the Japanese classify bonsai by size. The very smallest bonsai are known as "miniatures" and often occupy pots not much larger than an oversize thimble. The next gradation is the "mame" bonsai which, literally in Japanese, means "palm size." Next come the medium bonsai from six to twelve-inches tall and, beyond that, are the two-man and four-man giants.

How small or how large a bonsai should be depends on the grower's tastes. But, sooner or later, the average grower wants something *big*. First, our friend will browse the garden. If one makes covetous overtures at something suitable that was planted when the house was built, one will receive unpleasant glances from the spouse of the household—and one wouldn't dare! Next the enthusiast will scour the nurseries only to find that a substantial trunk and strong surface roots occur in a tree too tall for pleasing branch placement and proportion. The first branch would have to be about three-quarters of the way up the trunk.

In desperation, the enthusiast will plan on a collecting expedition and, by this time, the die is cast. There is going to be a big one! If a rootball of seventy-five or eighty pounds can be managed—if patience to nurture this tree for two or three years or more can be assured—and gradual transfer of the specimen from the ground, to a tub, to a large wood box, to a smaller box and, eventually, to a ceramic pot can be accomplished—the heart's desire will be attained. But it's a long, hard pull and disappointment is one of the perils.

**The longing never ends.**    There is always the craving for just one more, the perfect specimen. It's the perfectionist reaching for the stars. The next one will be better—and so will the next!

Then, there are those who suffer a malady the author diagnosed as "Potting Panic." A specimen can be studied for weeks or months in anticipation of the styling. Then the season arrives. On the appointed day, the tree is styled in perfect tranquility and concentration. All the major pruning has been done. The beautiful surface roots have been exposed. Every unnecessary branch has been removed. Each remaining branch carefully wired and bent to perfection. The trunk has an exquisite taper. Just wait until it is placed into that pot of perfect proportions. This is going to be it!

Alas, just as the tree is about to be positioned into the container, the artist falls apart. It's not that the stylist is concerned about the roots drying out, or that the material will not fit into the pot, or that the project will not be finished by dinner time. One becomes gripped with panic.

Now the planting is finished; you gape at the results in dismay. If only the tree were turned another 15° clockwise; why didn't I pot it just a little closer to the left? A fraction-of-an-inch higher in the pot would have been just right. Well, at the re-potting time next year, these things will be corrected—and just wait until you see it then.

The author has a feeling that "Potting Panic" is just another stage of the perfectionist syndrome. It's a very contagious malady. Maybe this is the thing that gets into your blood. Maybe this is as it should be.

# References

[1] NAKA, JOHN YOSHIO, *Bonsai Techniques,* Los Angeles, CA: Published for The Bonsai Institute of California by Dennis-Landman, Santa Monica, CA, 1973.

[2] YOSHIMURA, YUJI and HALFORD, GIOVANNA M., *The Japanese Art of Miniature Trees and Landscapes,* Rutland, VT and Tokyo: Charles E. Tuttle Co., 1957.

[3] KORESHOFF, DEBORAH R., *Bonsai, Its Art, Science, History and Philosophy.* Brisbane, Australia: Boolarong Publications: Timber Press, Portland, OR: Croom Helm, London: Macmillan South Africa, Johannesburg, 1984.

[4] YOUNG, DOROTHY S., *Bonsai, The Art and Technique,* Englewood Cliffs, NJ: Prentice-Hall, Inc., 1985.

[5] LESNIEWICZ, PAUL, *Bonsai, The Complete Guide to Art and Technique,* Poole, Dorset, England; Blandford Press: Sterling Publishing Co.: New York, NY, 1986.

[6] STOWELL, JERALD P, *The Beginner's Guide to American Bonsai,* Tokyo: Kodansha International Ltd and New York, NY: Kodansha International/USA, 1978.

[7] MURATA, KYUZO, *Bonsai Miniature Potted Trees,* Tokyo: Shufunotomo Co., Ltd., 1978.

[8] MURATA, KEIJI and TAKEUCHI, TAKEMA, *Bonsai for Pleasure,* Tokyo: Japan Publications, Inc.: Japan Publications Trading Company: San Francisco, CA, 1969.

[9] SUN, WU-YEE, *Man Lung Artistic Pot Plants,* Hong Kong: Wing Lung Bank Ltd., 1976.

PETRIDES, GEORGE A., *A Field Guide to Trees and Shrubs,* Boston, Mass.: Houghton Mifflin Company, 1958. (For species identifications.)

(BULLETIN) International Minerals & Chemical Corp.. Mundelein, Ill. (For technical details, *Turface*)

*Indoor Gardening:* United States Department of Agriculture, Home and Garden Bulletin No. 220 (For "Indoor Bonsai").

NICHOLS, LESTER P., *Tree Diseases, Description and Control,* University Park, PA: Pennsylvania State University, Cooperative Extension. ("Pest Control").

KETCHLEDGE, EDWIN H., *Mosses—Our Unseen Friends:* New York State College of Forestry, Syracuse. NY: New York State Conservationist, Syracuse. NY. 1961. (For "Moss & Lichen").

LOWE, JOSIAH L., *Some Lichens of New York:* New York State College of Forestry, Syracuse. NY: New York State Conservationist, Syracuse. NY. 1961. (For "Moss & Lichen").

Cooperative Extension Bulletin, Cornell University. State University of New York. Ithaca, NY: *Dormant Spraying of Ornamental Trees and Shrubs.*

KLOSS, CAROLYN and RAFFENSPERGER. ED. *Cooperative Extension Bulletin.* Department of Entomology, Cornell University. "Pesticides." 1986.

# Addenda

## POTTING

**Positioning surface roots.** If you have attractive surface roots on only one side of the trunk, try to position the tree in the pot so these roots are visible from the front view. So often it happens that priceless surface roots are relegated to the back, unobserved, because the front of the planting was decided too quickly. Look at the plant from all angles before selecting the front view.

**Moisture insurance.** Before potting a specimen from a nursery can or balled and bagged stock, water it thoroughly at least an hour before the potting procedure. This will create a reservoir of moisture within the plant tissues until the fibrous roots can function and take over on their own. Placing newly-potted bonsai in shade for one week after potting also checks moisture loss at a critical time. Anything you can do to prevent dehydration after potting will enhance the survival rate and forestall die-back.

## REPOTTING

**The Timing.** Some growers just pick their best plants to repot first, then they procrastinate again with other favorites before considering the problem specimens. The best way to determine whether repotting is necessary is to lift the ball out of the pot and examine the ball for radiating roots (see page 42).

Assuming, after an inspection, that the rootage of a particular plant is overgrown and potbound, the next step is to determine which species to tackle first. The best clues come from growing signals of the plants themselves. Deciduous species are re-potted just as buds start to break through; next come pines when candles appear but before they elongate; then come spruces when branch tips are still light green; box varieties are re-potted next when the first surge of new growth appears (early spring); finally, repot other conifers (juniper and cypress) and, last, broad-leaf species (azalea).

**Procedure.** Comb out the roots with a chopstick so they are suspended and easy to trim with scissors. Like the first potting, make sure all exposed roots contact new soil. Allow a few untrimmed roots to remain.

If there is enough ballast in the rootball to hold the trimmed ball in the container, it is unnecessary to secure the ball with wire. Complete the potting sequence as with the first potting. Trim the foliage lightly.

**Repotting crisis.** Sometimes a bonsai becomes so potbound and the soil so compacted, the rootball resembles a mass of hardpan. It is almost impossible to free the rootball from the pot short of using a crowbar.

Repotting obviously had been delayed too long. Extensive root pruning is the penalty for severely potbound root systems in contrast to the moderate trimming that ordinarily would be required.

An alternative to a crisis-potting situation is to spread the procedure over two seasons. Prune overgrown roots and trim the top moderately the first season; repeat the procedure the next season. This will restore the growth balance, but styling development will have been delayed one year.

It is not such a big chore to repot regularly. It becomes a project with uncertainty when repotting is neglected.

**Repotting false alarm.** Sometimes a bonsai does not appear to be doing well with new, active growth and good color. This may suggest repotting. An examination of the roots, however, does not indicate overgrowth. In fact, the roots may appear as if they failed to develop at all. In this situation, you can suspect faulty drainage. Repot the specimen with very light root pruning. Use a soil medium with superior drainage capability and one that will be appropriate to the pot size and plant species (see "Soils," page 51).

**Repotting reminders.**
—Always repot away from a location of direct wind and sunlight.
—Keep a spray bottle handy to moisten roots periodically during the repotting procedure. Add a drop of Superthrive to the spray water.
—If the rootball appears frozen to the pot, loosen the sides with a flat blade. If the rootball still resists removal, drench the ball with water and lift at the same time to dislodge the bottom.
—Make a list beforehand of all the things you intend to correct such as shifting position, branches to be removed, tilting changes, corrections involving wiring and soil adjustments to modify drainage. It is so easy to forget important styling changes.

## POTTING SOILS

**Humus, compost, leafmold.** These soil conditioners all are derived from the same sources—decayed organic matter that has aged and decomposed. The conditioners are formed through the decay of plants, roots, insects and the remains of small animals. Decay is caused through the action of bacteria and fungi. The identifying terms are used interchangeably.

*Humus* is the result of composting, either naturally through accumulated litter on the forest floor, or man-made from the compost pile; *compost* is the end result of the composting process; when tree foliage is the principal source of the reaction, it is known as *leafmold*. Regardless of the sources, the end results are the same and they are used for the same purpose—soil conditioning. These soil components are not substitutes for fertilizers, but they do introduce organic matter into the soil which is a factor when synthetic mixes are used (See *Synthetic Mixes and Fertilizing,* page 56).

Other forms of compost are peat moss, ground bark (also identified as "Orchid Seedling Soil") and dehydrated cow manure.

**Soil mesh for small pots.**    For containers less than two-inches deep (see Soil Meshes, page 55), greater *moisture retention* is required. For these shallow containers, use only the builders sand rather than half-and-half builders and acquarium sand; for the main potting component, use garden loam or Turface that passes through the $1/16$-inch screen and remains on the $1/32$-inch screen.

STYLING

**Determine the cause of a loss.**    When you lose a branch, do a perfunctory post-mortem. If the branch was wired, carefully remove the coil. See if there might have been a break in the bark caused by wiring, or a break in the internode caused by bending. Note the color of the foliage. Branches from deciduous bonsai expire quickly after an injury; conifers hold needles for weeks after a branch dies.

If a plant in stress is a juniper and the foliage looks gray, suspect spider mite. Infestations are common in August and September. Also, junipers sometimes lose branches for no apparent reason while other portions of the tree may flourish. In these situations, determine whether the lost branch might have been shaded by a branch above. If a branch loses color gradually you can suspect insufficient light.

Try to pinpoint the cause for the lost branch. It will help to learn what to avoid in the future.

**Ageing clue.**    An important characteristic of long life is the terminal. Old trees invariably develop a rounded apex rather than a pointed one—a crown-like shape rather than a spire. As the terminal slows in growth due to the ageing process, lateral branches become dominant, the bark more rugged.

**Details for multiple-trunk styles.**    Remove branches between trunks. Avoid opposite branching on adjacent trunks the same as single trunk plantings. Stagger lateral branches at different levels when observed from the front. Each trunk should have a back branch emerging at a different level. Vary the tree heights and, ideally, trunk thicknesses.

**Permissive deception.**    It is not always possible, even after a bonsai has received impeccable styling attention, for every element to fall into perfect alignment. Sometimes a branch is lost and creates a gap in the design, or a surrogate terminal fails to develop as envisioned. Sometimes it becomes necessary to "cover up" a blemish in design by wiring or shaping a branch to conceal rather than to enhance. Is this deception? No. This becomes part of the artform. Concealing a flaw that might spoil the illusion is part of the artistry.

**Improving trunk thickness.**    Theories abound on how to fatten trunks on trees in containers. Planted in the ground, trunks expand noticeably; they grow about five times faster than potted specimens. This includes trunk thickness as well as tree height. In warm environments, this growth rate can be doubled. At least two or three seasons in the ground are the minimum for any significant change in trunk girth.

In the confined environment of a pot, bonsai grow slowly. If trunk diameter is apparent at all, the caliper is calculated in millimeters. By contrast, bonsai growing on black volcanic rock thickens appreciably (see Photo #5). The black color of the rock holds the heat of the sun and transfers heat to the plant's roots.

Low-branching allowed to grow rank will noticeably stimulate trunk thickness. The unwanted branches can be removed after results are apparent. Some growers keep "spare" branches exclusively for this purpose eventually sacrificing them for styling.

As trees grow taller in nature, they sway back and forth with the wind. In the process, the trunks expand. Nature strives to reinforce the trees by strengthening the trunks with extra girth—genetic self-defense. So there are those who seek to imitate nature by "wiggling" their bonsai daily to simulate wind.

The quest for thick trunks can be drawn to extremes when you consider the time required for remodeling or isolation in the ground—time that might better be devoted to training and styling.

While bonsai with strong, short trunks have unique appeal and are held in high regard by bonsai afficionados, more often than not those elements are well developed either in the wild or at the bonsai nursery long before the plants are acquired by the ultimate grower.

There are tricks and shortcuts in almost every artistic discipline, but no one can deny the salutory effect of *time* in delivering respectable trunk girth to bonsai.

**Dormancy and pruning.**    Deciduous species do not go into total dormancy until about sixty days after defoliation. Evergreens and broadleaf species retain foliage, but it discolors. Pines stay green all through dormancy. Each plant has a separate set of dormancy requirements which involve sunlight, temperature and a freezing period. These factors are coordinated before dormancy sets in, usually at 40° or lower.

Sometimes there is an urge to pinch, prune or cut back branches at the first sign of dormancy. Since branches are bare of leaves it is easy to see internodes and branch structure and growers want to get a head start on spring. It is still too soon. In the case of the deciduous trees, defoliation is only one clue to the state of dormancy.

Pruning before trees have settled into complete dormancy is risky. First, an unseasonable warm spell, while having no effect on unpruned branches, may force a premature bud break. This new, tender growth may die back at the first hard freeze because the pruning cut had no time to harden.

Second, premature pruning can set up stresses that will be apparent in the spring when the branch fails to bud out. The hormone that regulates budding accumulates at branch tips during the dormancy cycle. As long as this hormone is in place, it keeps buds dormant until they are ready to emerge when spring temperature and sunlight are suitable. When a branch tip is cut prematurely, the growth hormone is also removed and the branch receives the wrong signals. The result is premature budding and possible die-back.

Conclusion: The best time to prune any branch is when new growth is apparent in early spring, after a full period of dormancy when the presence of hormones at branch tips keeps the buds in check until they are ready to emerge.

CARE

**Spooled wire.**    Copper wire purchased in spools must be re-wound to a larger coil for annealing. Wind the wire around a coffee can. Place the new coil in the charcoal burner.

**Beware hot water hoses.**    If the watering hose laying on the ground bakes in the sun, the water coming out of the nozzle can be heated up to as much as 180°. This can spell doom to tender plant species. When a hose is stored on the ground in full sun, allow water to flush through before applying it. Test the water temperature with your hand.

**Insecticide update.**    Insecticidal soap works by contact rather than systemically. It is most effective for soft-bodied insects such as aphid, mealy bug, spider mite and some caterpillars such as tent caterpillar when applied early in the growth cycle. The pests must be thoroughly doused. For maximum effect, the soap solution should be allowed to dry slowly. Spray early in the morning or during humid weather.

# Index